Speak to the Earth

A Healing the Land Handbook

Rev. Qaumaniq Suuqiina and Dr. I. Suuqiina

ISBN #: 0967379106

Previously released in 1999 as _"Can You Feel the Mountains Tremble?"_

IMI Publishing

P.O.Box 1088

Victorville, CA 92393

nidgenus@cs.com or www.IndigenousMessengers.com

All scripture quotations from The Scriptures, Institute for

Scripture Research P.O.Box 1830 2162 Northriding

Republic of South Africa –reprinted 2002, unless otherwise noted.

Cover art "Lone Tree" –oil by Suuqiina

Table of Contents

page 3 – Acknowledgements

4 – Introduction

17 – Chapter One – YHWH Loves the Land

41 – Chapter Two – What Defiles the Land?

57 – Chapter Three – Speak to the Earth

66 – Chapter Four – Keeping the Gates

82 – Chapter Five – Spiritual Mapping

91 – Chapter Six – The Presence of YHWH

103 – Chapter Seven – Breaking Strongholds

114- Chapter Eight – Indigenous Peoples

127 – Chapter Nine – To The Nations

132 – Appendix A – Blessings of thanks for the earth

133 – Appendix B – Sample Prayer

135 – Appendix C – A Warning

137 – Appendix D – Instructions for Prayer-Walks

138 – Appendix E – Excerpts from Culture, Christ, & Kingdom Seminar

153 – Appendix F – Additional Resources

154 – Appendix G – IMI Resources

Acknowledgements

Quyana Agaayun (thank you YHWH) for making this great land and all our relations on it!

To write thoughts, even good thoughts, is an awesome task. What can easily be spoken doesn't always appear the same in print. No one is born an author and we weren't either. Our struggle to rewrite *Can You Feel the Mountains Tremble?* (this book's original title) was constant and it was tempting to grow weary along the way. Thanks to those who persisted in asking for a revised version and encouraging us to complete this enhanced and expanded version.

Thanks to our families for their love, patience, and support!

Thanks to those in ministry for keeping open hearts and minds to our message.

Thanks to our relations, the First Nations Peoples across this great land. Your struggles, tears, and prayers have not gone unnoticed or unanswered. Our land is being healed! We join our hearts to your prayers, hopes, and dreams that we will come into the complete fulfillment of our destiny which the Creator had for us from the beginning. Keep drumming, dancing, and singing until the Great Spirit's love flute blows in the sky above and calls us home.

Thanks to our friends, and we are blessed to be able to count so many. You have blessed our lives by your friendship, fellowship, and teachable hearts.

Thanks to our IMI Board Members and Vision Team. Your support and prayers have kept us "on-the-road" for a long time now. Keep up the good work!

Thanks to those who have gone before us and made a way for us to heal this land! Often they struggled with a vision they could barely see, a word they could barely hear, and a song they could barely sing. They struggled onward hoping the following generations would not fail them. Anything of real value is worth their struggle. They enabled us to give a good account to Creator concerning His land.

Our Creator Elohim spoke (native and Hebrew tradition indicates He sang) this great land into existence and gifted mankind with stewardship of the earth. It is a sacred trust. We say, "Thank you, Great Mystery, for trusting mankind with Your creation."

Introduction

"The answer is not just adopting any old religious view; it is individual, national, and global repentance. And in that costly but centrally essential act lies the moral key to the ecological crisis." Winkie Pratney

Pratney,Winkie,*Healing the Land*(Grand Rapids,MI:Chosen Books,1993),p.56

"If I shut up the heavens and there is no rain, or if I command the locust to devour the land, or if I send pestilence among My people, and My people upon whom My Name is called, shall humble themselves, and pray and seek My face, and turn from their evil ways, then I shall hear from heaven, and forgive their sin and ***heal their land***."

2 Chronicles 7:13-14 (emphasis mine)

"God's calling the Christian now and to the Christian community in the area of nature is that we should exhibit now a substantial healing between man and nature and nature and it self as far as Christians can bring it to pass."

Dr. Francis Schaeffer, ibid., Pratney

"We shall continue to have a worsening ecological crisis until we reject the Christian axiom that nature has no reason for existence but to serve man...Both our present science and technology are so tinctured with orthodox Christian arrogance towards nature that no solution for our ecological crisis can be expected from them alone. Since the roots of our troubles are so largely religious, the remedy also must be essentially religious, whether we call it so or not." Lynn White

White,L. 1967. 'Historical Roots of our Ecological Crisis',*Science* pp.1203-7

Breaking Chains — *oil by Sungüna*

"To live we must daily break the body and shed the blood of creation. When we do this knowingly, lovingly, skillfully and reverently, it is a sacrament. When we do it ignorantly, greedily, clumsily, and destructively, it is a desecration. In such a desecration we condemn ourselves to spiritual moral loneliness and others to want." Wendell Berry

Berry, Wendell.*The Gift of Good Land*, Op.cit.North Point Press, P.281

"We must convince each generation that they are transient passengers on this planet earth. It does not belong to them. They are not free to doom generations yet unborn. They are not at liberty to erase humanity's past nor dim its future." Bernard Lown and Evjueni Chazov

Quoted in *Peace, A Dream Unfolding*, P.Crean and P.Kome,eds.

To become human, one must make room in oneself for the wonders of the universe. South American Indigenous Proverb

"As scientists, many of us have had no profound experience of awe and reverence before the universe. We understand that what is regarded as sacred is more likely to be treated with care and respect. Our planetary home should be so regarded. Efforts to safeguard and cherish the environment need to be infused with a vision of the sacred,"

Union of Concerned Scientists, Joint Commitment in Science and Religion

"As civilization advances, the sense of wonder declines. Such decline is an alarming symptom of our state of mind. We will not perish for want of information, but only for want of appreciation." Rabbi Abraham Joshua Heschel

Jeremy Bernstein, *The Way Into Judaism and the Environment,*

Jewish Lights Publishing, Woodstock, VT 05091

The holy scriptures present 1747 verses that reference or speak of the land. The land is important to Elohim. But there's a problem with the land. It is groaning, crying, and shrieking in distress. This handbook tells us what the problem is, how to correct it, and offers some solutions on how to heal the land. It is impossible to cover, in depth, every ecological circumstance, but general principles are transferable to most local situations. Elohim has given us a window of opportunity to heal the land before He returns and calls us to account for our stewardship. Let's be wise and use our limited time for our sake, our children's sake, and the sake of all beings and the land itself.

"If you want to heal the land, begin with the furrowing of your own heart and cry out to God for His mercy on our poor and broken creation. But above all, "do the right thing" first. Do not speak of guarding a clean earth with a dirty heart and an idolatry polluted soul. Do not ask for the blessing of heaven when you have every intention of living like hell. Get your own soul right with the living God. Get the ground of your life broken up, watered with tears, sown in righteousness. Become a man or woman God can trust with the care of His creation."

Winkie Pratney, Ibid., pp.175,170

A "furrowing" must include some admission that a "new Gnosticism" has arisen within the believing community that shuns the earth in favor of a theology that is "spiritualistic" and "futuristic." This so-called "spirituality" fosters an increasing insistence upon so-called "spiritual events" that largely ignore the "lesser" things of the earth including ecological stewardship. Such stewardship, for many "believers," is thought to be "new age" and/or "liberal politics."

It seems interesting that many conservatives have difficulty with conservation. The acceptance of a theology of the "future" tends to set aside present problems, even those in crisis proportions, as an unnecessary burden and for which no individual need take specific measures of personal responsibility. If we are really going to be "outta-here" (the rapture eschatology), why take on such "mundane" and "unimportant" issues such as pollution, idolatry, ecology, or healing the land?

We encourage everyone to heal the land (as much as possible) of their own lives BEFORE attempting to heal the land outside of them. Personal histories may have to be researched, understood, and embraced for the necessary integrity to have real and lasting impact upon the land. Personal repentance (in Hebrew *teshuva* which means to behave differently not simply think differently), reconciliation, restoration, and relationships may have to be examined and integrated into one's life. Blame-shifting must be rooted out of one's life and thinking process and replaced with response-ability.

This stewardship of the earth must be viewed and embraced as a sacred trust. It is part of what it means to be a spiritual being having a human experience. It is included in the reality of being a believer and follower of the Creator, Elohim. It cannot be ignored and it should not be diminished. The popular dualism of "sacred vs. secular" must be eliminated from our thinking and replaced with a holistic view of ourselves and the world around us. Everything in nature is sacred because the One who made it is sacred. Most First Nations peoples have this worldview and it guides them towards a healthy stewardship attitude and practice.

As a native, I might say something like, "All people are my relations and all living things are my companions." Some Westerners may feel uncomfortable with such thought and may think I'm leaning toward pantheism or nature worship. This is not pantheism. There are differences in nature that cannot be denied, but there is a similarity, through our mutual Creator, which cannot be ignored. Begin to explore the sacredness of nature. Let the earth speak to you. Let the stars prophesy knowledge (see Psalm 19) and allow creation to reveal, clearly, the nature of the Creator by the things He has made (Romans 1:20).

As we listen to the songbirds, the croaking frogs, the barking dogs, the howling wolves, or the huffing bison, does not the scripture, "Let everything that has breath bless YHWH" apply equally to creature-kind as well as mankind?

Letter by Chief Seattle

Chief Seattle wrote a letter to the American President in 1854 in response to a request by the government to purchase the Indian (Duwamish) lands and relocate the tribe to a reservation (a little over 300 acres). The letter doesn't focus on the economic value of the land or haggle over the price. Chief Seattle's concern is about what will happen to the land.

"How can you buy or sell the sky, the warmth of the land? The idea is strange to us. If we do not own the freshness of the air and the sparkle of the water, how can you buy them?

Every part of the earth is sacred to my people. Every shining pine needle, every sandy shore, every mist in the dark woods, every clearing and humming insect is holy in the memory and experience of my people. The sap which courses through the trees carries the memories of the red man. The white man's dead forget the country of their birth when they go to walk among the stars. Our dead never forget this beautiful earth, for it is the mother of the red man. We are part of the earth and it is part of us. The perfumed flowers are our sisters; the deer, the horse, the great eagle, these are our brothers. The rocky crests, the juices in the meadows, the body heat of the pony, and man – all belongs to the same family.

So, when the great Chief in Washington sends word that he wishes to buy our land, he asks much of us. The great Chief sends word he will reserve us a place so that we can live comfortably among our own people. He will be our Father and we will be his children. So we will consider your offer to buy our land. But it will not be easy. For this land is sacred to us.

The shining water that moves in the streams and rivers is not just water but the blood of our ancestors. If we sell you our land, you must remember that it is sacred, and you must teach your children that each ghostly reflection in the clear water of the lakes tell of events and memories in the life of my people. The water's murmur is the voice of the father's father.

The rivers are our brothers, they quench our thirst. The rivers carry our canoes, and feed our children. If we sell you our land, you must remember, and teach your children, that the rivers are our brothers, and yours, and you must henceforth give the rivers the kindness you would give a brother.

We know the white man does not understand our ways. One portion of land is the same to him as the next, for he is a stranger who comes in the night and takes from the land whatever he needs. The earth is not his brother, but his enemy, when he has conquered it, he moves on. He leaves his father's graves behind, and he does not care. He kidnaps the earth from his children, and he does not care. His father's grave, and his children's birthright are forgotten. He treats his mother, the earth, and his brother, the sky, as things to be bought, plundered, sold like sheep or bright beads. His appetite will devour the earth and leave behind only desert.

I do not know. Our ways are different from yours. The sight of your cities pains the eyes of the red man. But perhaps it is because the red man is a savage and does not understand. There is no quiet place in the white man's cities; no place to hear the unfurling of leaves in the spring, or the rustle of the insect's wings. The clatter only seems to insult the ears. And what is there to life if a man cannot hear the lonely cry of the whipoorwill, or the arguments of frogs around a pond at night? The Indian prefers the soft sounds of the wind darting over the face of the pond, and the smell of wind itself, cleansed by the midday rain, or scented with the pinion tree.

The air is precious to the red man, for all things share the same breath – the beast, the tree, and the human. The white man does not seem to notice the air he breathes. Like a man dying for many days he is numb to the stench. But if we sell you our land you must remember that the air is precious to us, that the air shares its spirit with all the life it supports. The wind that gave our grandfathers his first breath also receives his last sigh. And if we sell you our land, you must keep it apart and sacred, as a place where even the white man can go to taste the wind that is sweetened by the meadow's flowers.

So we will consider your offer to buy our land. If we decide to accept it, I will make one condition; the white man must treat the beasts of this land as his brothers. I have seen a thousand rotting buffaloes on the prairie, left by the white man who shot them from a passing train. I am a savage and I do not understand how the smoking iron horse can be more important than the buffalo that we kill only to stay alive. What is man without the beasts? If all the beasts were gone, man would die from great loneliness of spirit, for whatever happens to the beasts also happens to man. All things are connected. Whatever befalls the earth befalls the sons of earth. The white man, too, shall pass-perhaps sooner than other tribes. Continue to contaminate your bed, and you will one night suffocate in your own waste. When the buffalo are all slaughtered, the wild horses tamed, the secret corners of the forest heavy with the scent of many men, and the view of ripe hills blotted out by talking wires, where is the thicket? Gone. Where is the eagle? Gone. And what is it to say goodbye to the swift pony and the hunt? It is the end of living and the beginning of survival."

Chief Seattle's letter has become an accurate, if not frightening, prophecy about the hearts and minds of many concerning the stewardship of the earth.

Vine Deloria writing in God is Red, recalls that Cayuse Indian Young Chief refused to sign the Treaty of Walla Walla because the wider creation was not properly represented and protected.

(see Deloria,Vine, *God is Red*(New York, A Laurel Book, Dell Publishing Co., 1973)

Over a life span it becomes necessary, many times, to take a peek outside the box of our own limited worldview and familiar paradigm. A heart and mind rooted in arrogance cannot lift the head long enough or far enough for such a peek to occur. **Healing the land is ultimately a call to humility.** There are many ways to look at all of this. Although you are reading this book, you will also need to look outside the books and Western affirmed sources and observe the whole of creation; your reliance upon it, your debt to it, and your responsibility to it.

The indigenous people of the earth, for the most part, have been viewed as savage barbarians who know little, if anything, about "proper" stewardship of the earth. That is because the Western societies have demonized such people and have been ignorant of their values and customs.

In 1887, Senator Dawes introduced "The Dawes (Allotment) Act" with the stated purpose of "....breaking up the tribal land mass." This is after the Indians had been removed from their traditional and divinely given inheritance and placed on reservations. Their boundaries were being moved again. Beyond the manipulation of getting more land for non-natives, the value Senator Dawes was promoting was the creation of unhindered greed. He is quoted in <u>*Blood of the Land*</u> by Rex Weyler:

"The head chief [of the Cherokees] told us that there was not a family in that whole nation that had not a home of its own. There was not a pauper nation, and the nation did not owe a dollar...Yet the defect of the system was apparent. They [the Indians} have got as far as they can go, because they own the land in common...There is no enterprise to make your home any better than that of your neighbor's. **There is no selfishness, which is at the bottom of civilization** (emphasis mine). Until this people consent to give up their lands and divide them among their citizens so that each can own land he cultivates, they will not make much progress."

Mander,Jerry *In the Absence of the Sacred*(Sierra Club Books,1991),p.276

There is an idea that appears subversive to Western society and the entire technological direction of the past century namely this – <u>reverence for the earth.</u> Without it and without reverence for all people of the earth, our actions and attitudes are fatally flawed.

Read this excerpt from *A Basic Call to Consciousness, the Hau de no sau nee* [Iroquoise] *Address to the Western World,* delivered at the 1977 United Nations Conference on Indigenous Peoples, published by *Akwesasne Notes:*

"In the beginning we were told that the human beings who walk about on the earth have been provided with all things necessary for life. We were instructed to carry a love for one another, and to show a great respect for all beings of the earth. We were shown that our life exists with the tree of life, that our well-being depends on the well-being of the vegetable life, that we are close relatives of the four-legged beings.

The original instructions direct that we who walk about on earth are to express a great respect, an affection for and a gratitude toward all the spirits which create and support life. When people cease to respect and express gratitude for these many things, then all life will be destroyed, and human life on this planet will come to an end.

The Indo-European people who have colonized our lands have shown very little respect for the things that create and support life. We believe that these people ceased their respect for the world a long time ago. Many thousands of years ago, all the people of the world believed the same Way of Life, that of harmony with the Universe. All lived according to the Natural ways.

Today the [human] species of Man is facing a question of [its] survival. The way of life known as Western Civilization is on a death path on which their own culture has no viable answers. When faced with the reality of their own destructiveness, they can only go forward into areas of more efficient destruction.

The air is foul, the waters poisoned, the trees dying, the animals disappearing. We think even the systems of weather are changing. Our ancient teaching warned us that if man interfered with the natural laws, these things would come to be. When the last of the natural way of life is gone, all hope for human survival will be gone with it. And our way of life is disappearing, a victim of the destructive process.

The technologies and social systems which destroyed the animal and the plant life are destroying the Native people. We know there are many people in the world who can quickly grasp the intent of our message. But our experience has taught us that there are few who are willing to seek out a method for moving toward any real change.

The majority of the world does not find its roots in Western culture or tradition. The majority of the world finds its roots in the natural world, and it is the natural world, and the traditions of the natural world, which must prevail.

We must all consciously and continuously challenge every model, every program, and every process that the West tries to force upon us. The people who are living on this planet need to break the narrow concept of human liberation, and begin to see liberation as something that needs to be extended to the whole of the natural world. What is needed is the liberation of all things that support life – the air, the waters, the trees – all things which support the sacred web of life.

The traditional native people hold the key to the reversal of the processes in Western civilization, which hold the promise of unimaginable future suffering and destruction. Spiritualism is the highest form of political consciousness. And we, the native people of the Western hemisphere, are among the world's surviving proprietors of that kind of consciousness. Our culture is among the most ancient continuously existing cultures in the world. We are the spiritual guardians of this place. We are here to impart that message."

Jerry Mander, ibid.pp191-192

So it comes down to greed versus reverence for life and for the earth. Some problems associated with greed is its ability to control human desires and designs, to accumulate economic power, to manifest political influence, to invent "progress," to assert the lies of its "virtues," but most destructively, to deride those values, traditional and spiritual, which expose greed for its own evil and perverted ways.

Many non-natives accuse, wrongly, natives of "worshipping" the land. Nothing could be further from the truth. Everything is sacred because, and only because, the One (YHWH) who created everything is sacred. He breathed sacred DNA into everything He created. There continues to exist, however, many cultural and social clashes because of these differing values, worldviews, and life practices. A Shoshone Native, Joe Sanchez, addresses the difficulty many Westerners have grasping the Indian struggles:

"For most Americans, land is a dead thing. It means nothing. But to disconnect from the land is unthinkable to Indians. The land is everything. It's the source of our existence. It's where the ancestor's spirits live. It is not a commodity that can be bought or sold, and to rip it open to mine is deeply sacrilegious to all Indian people. Nowadays most Americans live in or near cities. They have no connection with the dirt, with the earth. They have no way of identifying with the most essential feelings that define Indian experience or values. So they don't take us seriously. When our elders try to explain that Indian people die if they are removed from the land, Americans don't know what they are talking about. The schools and media don't help. The public pretty much assumes we're all dead and gone. We are invisible to Americans and so are our causes. To Americans we are just part of some story about the past, somehow connected to their own pioneer's heroics."

Jerry Mander, ibid.p.223

In his book, author David Suzuki writes:

"Here in the West we have exorcised the spirits and cut ourselves loose from the living web of the world. Instead of seeing ourselves as physically and spiritually connected to family, clan and land, we now live chiefly by the mind, as separate individuals acting on and relating to other separate individuals and on a lifeless, dumb world beyond the body. Applying our mind to the matter around us, we have produced an extraordinary material culture: cities and highways, toasters and blenders, computer technology, paper clips, assault rifles and television sets. But we find ourselves separated, fragmented, lonely, and fearful of death. We have coined a word for this state of mind: "alienation," which means being estranged. We are strangers in the world; we no longer belong. Because it is separate from us we can act on it, abstract from it, use it, take it apart; we can wreck it, because it is another, it is alien. We may feel despair, grief and guilt about the damage we cause- but we seem unable to change the way we live. How has this happened? Is it because we have lost our religion? Or is that a consequence rather than a cause? Perhaps it is the inevitable consequence of "modernization," as human societies have moved away from immediate dependence upon the land."

Suzuki,David, *The Sacred Balance* (Vancouver,BC.Greystone Books,1997),p.191

Any healing of the land that has real and lasting value will be life changing. *(i.e. The majority of the bee colony collapse disorder has been caused by cell-phone frequencies-would you give up yours for future pollination?*) Beliefs, thoughts, ideas, values, and life-ways will have to be truly examined and the dark corners of our hearts, where greed and selfishness reside, will have to be exposed to the light, not just any light, but cosmic light. The kind the Creator breathed into the universe and by which He lights "every man that comes into the world (see John 1)."

"The path of truth is laid out before us in the scriptures of the cosmos. Many scholars confine their study of the true ways to books but I find the fullness of truth written in the heavens and the earth. Human beings should open their eyes and read this book of the cosmos in order to seek the truth therein." *To Care for the Earth*, p.152

A Hebrew poet expressed it this way:

"The heavens are proclaiming the esteem of El; and the expanse is declaring the work of His hand.

Day to day pours forth speech, and night to night reveals knowledge.

There is no speech, and there are no words, where their voice is not heard.

Their line has gone out through all the earth, and their words to the end of the world.

In them He set up a tent for the sun, and it is like a bridegroom coming out of his room,

It rejoices like a strong man to run the path,

Its rising is from one end of the heavens, and its circuit to the other end;

And naught is hidden from its heat."

Tehillim (Psalms) 19:1-6

True spirituality, not Gnosticism; an understanding of present reality, not a strict adherence to futurism; humility not arrogance; and a larger cosmic view instead of a localized one is what is required for the depth of stewardship that heals the land.

A simple plan of action

Walk your neighborhood and note the beauty, the potential beauty, the pollution or trash that needs cleaned up.

Organize a neighborhood walk thru and clean up party.

Prayer- walk your neighborhood without intruding upon others or their property – it's a stealth thing.

Inventory your own views and values about YHWH's earth.

Have a family discussion about these things.

Chapter One

YHWH Loves the Land

"The whole difference between construction and creation is exactly this; that a thing constructed can only be loved after it is constructed; but a thing created is loved before it exists."

G.K.Chesterton

W.Pratney, ibid.p.19

"...the whole land has been laid waste, because no one cares." Jeremiah12:11 New Life Version

YHWH loves the land so much He was able to create mankind out of it. The soil He created He called "Good." The dirt-man formed from the soil He called "Very Good." Mankind is YHWH's land as much as the remaining earth soil. **The Creator made nothing evil in its original state.** Every purpose for everything was pure in its intention and design.

The Hebrew the words *b'reshiyt* (Genesis) and *bara* (created) contain the letters *beit* (B) and *resh* (R); the Hebrew word *bar* means pure, purity, and pureness (also used for wheat and barley). The beginning and the subsequent creation were both pure indicating there was no built-in defect. Mankind did not have to sin; mankind chose to sin. Mankind is not forced to defile, pollute, ruin, or harm the land. If mankind were to again love the land like his Creator, he must first embrace YHWH's kind of love for the land and the creation upon it.

It has become almost impossible for disciples of Yeshua the Messiah to express their concern and love for the land without being labeled as radical environmentalists or worse, as idolaters of it. From the scriptures it is clear that YHWH loves the land but His environmental concerns are not tainted by economic or political agendas. Nor are His affections rooted in some mystical spiritualism that is contaminated by carnal ceremony or empty emotionalism. He loves the land simply and only because He loves, as the Creator, the things He created. Everything created has lovingly designed purpose and His desire is for that purpose to be fulfilled. When His purposes are manifested in the earth, glory accrues to His name. He stated that His purpose for the land is for it to be fruitful and to produce everything necessary to provide, abundantly, for the whole of creation. ***YHWH is really into abundance!***

A person can experience a powerful emotion viewing the scenery around us. Without diminishing its importance and value, this book is not about scenic beauty. A person may have a fundamental respect for the property one owns and nurture its growth. This book is not about properties or their development. This book is about the actual, moral, spiritual, and purposeful stewardship of the whole earth; the land and the creatures upon it. It is about seeing the land in its current state versus its potential state for which YHWH designed it. It's about recognition of those things that defile the land and the consequences such defilements have on everyone and everything.

Because "sowing and reaping" is true, obedience like disobedience, purity like impurity, and respect like disrespect all contain elements of the future destinies for the earth. If the earth were to become spiritually, environmentally, and socially liberated, it would appear more attractive to everyone. It would produce more bountifully and provide better habitat for all creatures. Everyone's hearts would beat all the more at the thought of freeing and healing more land than their own. A nurturing attitude of stewardship would accumulate in the hearts and minds of many.

Mankind does not own the earth; mankind is the steward of it. Such stewardship includes both opportunity and responsibility.

"The heavens belong to YHWH. But He has given the earth to the children of men." Psalm 115:16

This gift from YHWH is the gift of stewardship.

Stewardship is defined as managing another's affairs or property.

Mankind has been gifted with high honor! The Creator trusts mankind with His creation. However, such honor and trust also include a time when the Owner requires an accounting of the management of his properties. This reckoning time is usually thought of in futuristic terms and time-tables. One principle this book encourages us to understand is that mankind can have a continuing stewardship and a constant accountability by obedience to the instructions (Torah= a Father's instructions) the Creator has given. We encourage readers to daily practice healing the land of their own bodies and their properties and communities.

YHWH is Owner

YHWH existed before the heavens and the earth which means He is different (*Kadosh* = holy or different, separate) from the things He created. He is the First (*Aleph*) and the Last (*Tav*) but His creation, including heavenly created beings, are not <u>coequal</u> with Him. YHWH is the Owner because He created everything by Himself and for Himself without permission from someone or something outside of Himself (see also Rev.4:11).

In Genesis 1 verse 1 we note that Elohim created the *Aleph/Tav* (the Alphabet-22 letters by which He created everything) before He creates the "heavens and the earth." Since He is the First and the Last, the alphabet was created out of His own person, nature, and character. This alphabet contains, what He calls, "Spirit and life (see John 6:63)." The Hebrew alphabet is living letters and words; creative, powerful, meaningful, instructive, and purposeful. His strength is mighty and awesome and is beheld in creation.

"The earth belongs to YHWH, and all that fills it –

the world and those who dwell in it." Psalm 24:1

YHWH states His ownership over all creation, creatures, and cultures. Satan is not a creator and owns nothing except what is given him by disobedience and sinful behavior. Satan is not the equal opposite of YHWH. He is far beneath and is merely a prince with a domain consisting of air (Eph.2:2). He can only pervert, destroy, or harm what has already been created. Nothing belongs to Satan or his domain except what is given to him. YHWH, the only Creator, claims rightful ownership over everything and everyone.

"And the land is not to be sold beyond reclaim (forever), for
the land is Mine, *for you are sojourners and settlers with Me."*

Leviticus 25:23 (emphasis mine)

YHWH will never relinquish His ownership of the heavens and the earth. This truth establishes confidence and peace for everything He created.

When mankind gives away land, through defilement, there is immediate conflict that is termed "spiritual warfare." It is a conflict between He Who owns the land and those who claim to own it. The enemies of YHWH and mankind earnestly covet the land for themselves. Their desire is to build spiritual strongholds upon the land from which to deceive, destroy, and weaken the proper land stewards. YHWH purposes to retain the land for Himself and His stewards as a habitation for His creation, creatures, and, ultimately, Himself. The warfare that waged above us and in the unseen realms is largely about land or land issues, the effect of which mankind feels and which affects all creation.

No wonder Rabbi Shaul (commonly known as the Apostle Paul) would write in Ephesians 4:27, *"nor give place to the devil."* The Greek word for "place" is "topos" and it is defined as territory, jurisdiction, or land. That Greek word is used in English speaking settings for "topo maps," or for "topography."

The idea is a simple one – if land is given to Satan, he will build something on it which is called a "stronghold." A group of strongholds is assigned a demon prince and called a "principality," thus YHWH's instruction to not give Satan any ground. Remember, the only ground Satan is legally entitled to is ground given to him by disobedience, sin, and defilement. Satan has not been assigned stewardship over the earth nor is he an heir to it.

Where is Satan's place in the universe? The heavens belong to YHWH; the earth is given to mankind in stewardship; and the air or mid-heaven is assigned to Satan. The scriptures refer to him as "the prince of the power of the air (Ephesians 2:2)." His rightful place, until he and his demons are cast into hell, is between heaven and earth. Satan, however, is not satisfied to simply hurl accusations at the earth-stewards, but to displace mankind and even YHWH, and rule the earth by taking it one small piece at a time. It is time to retrieve the land and steward it properly, healing it of all natural and spiritual defilement.

Many of the monumental events revealed in the Book of Revelation are about land redemption and removal of spiritual squatters from it. The fierceness of the battles described in it indicates how serious YHWH and Satan are about the earth and its stewardship.

Mankind is not commencing a spiritual battle. We are joining one begun by Satan when he introduced chaos into the earth (Genesis 1:2) and by the disobedience of Adam. The unseen angels and demons are veterans of this conflict and have seen the land at its worst. It became so defiled that YHWH flooded (Hebrew =*mikvah/baptism*) it saving only Noah and his family.

We know YHWH is "slow to anger," "full of mercy," "abounding in long-suffering," but our servants, His angels, have to wonder why mankind continues to give huge chunks of land to Satan without giving much thought to the present or future consequences of their actions.

The land is seeking relief from the pressures of defilement and the sinful landlords who constantly terrorize the earth's tenants. As rightful stewards, mankind holds more authority than either angels or demons over the earth. This authority must be manifested with humility, repentance, and wisdom. The stakes are high for creation and all creatures. The stewardship of the earth is a sober responsibility requiring keen insights, astute hearing, correct observation, and a proper adherence to the instructions given in the earth manual (Tor

Psalm 24 – Ownership versus Stewardship

Verse 1 – *"The earth belongs to YHWH, and all that fills it – the world and those who dwell in it."*

YHWH is the Owner and this will never, ever change. Mankind needs to agree with this reality and not struggle against it. This verse reveals that there is no "godless place" anywhere on earth nor are there any "godless people." YHWH has not abandoned any place or any people. There are only two categories of people – believers and pre-believers. "Every knee will eventually bow" before their Owner.

Verse 2 – *"For He has founded it upon the seas, and upon the waters He does establish it."*

YHWH is the Creator and there exists no others. As Creator, He has created stewardship and all levels of authority, both natural and spiritual. YHWH has both the right and the power to accomplish these things. He will never weaken or diminish, through negotiation, threat, or coercion these rights and powers.

The use of waters in the scripture is abundant. In the beginning the earth was covered with water. In the Hebrew culture this is a *mikvah* (cleansing baptism). He washes the whole earth and calls forth many things from the waters including light (Genesis 1:3). After Noah's flood, YHWH promises to never flood the earth with water again.

Verse 3 – *"Who does go up into the mountain of YHWH? And who does stand in His set-apart (holy) place?"*

YHWH has established rights of access to His presence, His land, and His purposes. This access is controlled by gates and gate-keepers. Proper protocol is not set aside by the realities of redemption. He remains committed to order and the elimination of all vestiges of chaos.

Verse 4 – *"He who has innocent hands and a clean heart, who did not bring his life to naught, and did not swear deceivingly."*

When it comes to stewardship, holiness (being separate or different), truthfulness, and integrity rule. They become the passwords for the Gatekeeper to allow us access to YHWH's presence. It is precisely here that the gifts of humility and repentance can enter into our lives with strength and promise. YHWH rewards the humble. He responds to repentance (teshuva). His mercy and grace is ready to act on behalf of His stewards. He is not keeping us away but rather trying, earnestly, to draw us closer to His heart.

Verse 5 – *"He receives a blessing from YHWH, and righteousness from the Elohim of His deliverance."*

YHWH is generous with His handouts including righteousness (doing what is right with our fellowman). YHWH always has good things in mind for us, not bad things (see Jeremiah 29:11). Ultimately, His gifts include salvation and returning to favor with Him. He came to "seek and save the lost."

Verse 6 – *"This is the generation of those who seek Him; Jacob, who seek Your face. Selah."*

Stewardship is generational and carries forward from one generation to the next one. Stewardship is a "face-to-face" relationship with the Owner of the earth. Because of the promises in verses 4 and 5, this "face-to-face" encounter becomes meaningful and satisfying.

The conflict over the land has been expressed in the scriptures as a family event; Cain versus Able, Isaac versus Ishmael, and Esau versus Jacob. The very name Esau (Esauph) in scriptures means to waste, hairy, or the grass of the field. It is grass that has no nutrition, and is expressed as goat (hairy or Sier). Jacob is represented by the sheep and although he is humbled, he is given a new identity and a new name (Israel).

The scriptures identify Esau as a "profane (Latin – *profanum*, before the fane, the holy place) man." He was an "outer-court" or "before the *fane"* kind of person, not seeking the face of YHWH.

Jacob, with all his foibles, seeks to become a man of YHWH and follow in the generational footsteps of Abraham and Isaac. We are to be a "Jacob" generation.

Verse 7 – *"Lift up your heads, O you gates! And be lifted up, you everlasting doors! And let the Sovereign of esteem come in."*

Knowing our Creator through personal redemption and relationship, having access to His presence, and having a historical, generational foundation, earth stewards are able to address ecological, social and spiritual issues ushering in YHWH's presence, purposes, and deepest desires for mankind and His creatures. Before Adam and Eve disobeyed, they were stewards of the garden and experienced a daily entrance of YHWH's presence in their lives. ***Obedience is always a welcoming environment.***

Verse 8 – *"Who is this Sovereign of esteem? YHWH strong and mighty, YHWH mighty in battle."*

YHWH does not abandon mankind in their efforts to be proper stewards; He joins the battle. He acts with strength and might revealing His warrior attributes. He is able and willing to fight for what is rightfully His. Every steward of the earth is a warrior at some level. There is a significant battle over global manifestations of unbridled greed, power, and control and these are often is opposition to the values necessary to heal the land. In this fight for good dirt, those who *claim* authority will be distinguished from those who *have* authority. Any stewardship "wanna-be's" will not persevere in this battle. (This may be an excellent time to review what Rabbi Shaul wrote about the armor of YHWH in Ephesians 6.)

Verse 9, 10 – *"Lift up your heads, O you gates! Even lift up, you everlasting doors! And let the Sovereign of esteem come in. Who is this Sovereign of esteem? YHWH of Hosts, He is the Sovereign of esteem! Selah."*

YHWH desires and will make a habitation with His stewards; <u>He will not settle for a visitation</u>. The scriptures reveal His desire for close, personal, and proximate fellowship with His creation. He will "renew" the heavens and the earth." He only withdraws from the presence of disobedience, sin, and rebellion. YHWH, King of the Universe, has never lost a battle and when He wins, we also win! Both ownership and stewardship issues are real. They matter to YHWH and because they are important to Him, they ought also to be important to us.

Psalm 24 shows us the relationship that exists between the Owner and His stewards. The rights of access is revealed as inward character which provides availability to the promises of good and right things from YHWH. He founded our stewardship in generational history and He remains the "YHWH of Abraham, Isaac, and Jacob (Israel). He acts upon our cooperation of His ownership displaying His warrior attributes. This harmony of ownership and stewardship shows that YHWH has endowed us with His splendor. He has faith in mankind. However, negligence in stewardship forces YHWH to act in judgment upon the land and its inhabitants in negative ways. (Judgment is always a positive thing but it may be manifested in negative ways-YHWH operates with eternity in mind and not just for immediate results.)

Four Judgments upon the Land

Famine – *"Son of man, when a land sins against Me to commit a trespass, and I shall stretch out My hand against it, and cut off its supply of bread and send scarcity of food on it, and cut off man and beast from it..."* *Ezekiel 14:13*

History has never recorded a time when famine was not present somewhere on the earth. History has never recorded a time when sin was not present on the earth except for the duration of time when Adam and Eve were obedient to Abba's instructions (Torah). Famines are not simply the result of poor weather producing inadequate crops but they bear the marks of Divine intervention as judgment upon sin and trespass.

"When you looked for much, then see, it came to little. And when you brought it home, I would blow on it. "Why?" declares YHWH of hosts. "Because of My House which lies in ruins, while each of you runs to his own house. Therefore the heavens above you have withheld the dew, and the earth has withheld its fruit. And I called for a drought on the land, and on the mountains, and on the grain, and on the new wine, and on the oil, and on

whatever the ground brings forth, and on man, and on livestock, and on all the labor of the hands." Haggai 1:9-11

"And He called for a scarcity of food in the land; He cut off all the supply of bread." Psalm 105:16

In 2006, scientist began to report the rapid disappearance of bees around the world. This is a disturbing thing for all mankind. One third of the food we eat requires pollination from bees. Already we are seeing reports of food shortages from the lack of enough bees and hives. By 2011, the earth had lost 72% of its bees. The causes for Colony Collapse Disorder (CCD) were listed as virus, fungus, pesticides and a mite. The most significant cause, however, is the proliferation of cell phones and cell phone towers. Apparently, these technologies use the same frequencies which provide direction for bees returning to their hives after their collection of nectar and pollen. Mankind is actually precipitating a global famine by choosing progressive technology over the enormous provision of food bees naturally create.

Famine, as Divine Judgment, can arrest our attention and propel us toward the humility and repentance necessary to foment restoration of abundance and blessing.

"And after all this, if you do not obey Me, then I shall punish you seven times more for your sins. And I shall break the pride of your power, and shall make your heavens like iron and your earth like bronze. And your strength shall be spent in vain and your land will not yield its crops, nor the trees of the land yield their fruit." Leviticus 26:18-20

Charles Lynn said, "America cannot shrug off another drought and trust in technology instead of rain to deliver our fields. We can marvel that the scripture gives us Elijah as a model to set our sights on in prayer. A man or a people that can open or shut the windows of heaven are of utmost importance to a nation's life, economy and existence."

W.Pratney, ibid., p.148

Ecological Devastation

"If I cause an evil beast to pass through the land, and it shall bereave it, and it shall be a wasteland, so that no man passes through because of the beasts, even though these three men (Noah, Daniel, Job) were in it, as I live, "declares the Master YHWH, they would deliver neither sons nor daughters. They alone would be delivered, but the land would be a wasteland."

Ezekiel 14:15-16

Media headlines continue to announce the conflict man and animals experience simply because of the constant and increasing loss of habitat. Pollution and other kinds of destructive activities affect the arctic tundra, rain forest, rivers, and air. Animals don't always welcome encroachment upon their habitat and we increasingly hear reports of animal attacks upon humans. For instance, in Anchorage, Alaska, about 1,000 moose cohabitate with humans within the city limits and often there are violent conflicts, some even resulting in death.

Some animals are not on any endangered species list but are, in fact, on the rampage. Note the increase of "killer bees" in North America. We hear of ants, locusts, and flies making biblical kinds of appearances throughout the earth bringing devastation and disease. These reports will only increase.

With the human and technological intrusion into the vast rain forests of the Amazon Basin, we're now exposed to new viruses with no immunity developed yet. It appears impossible to reduce, much less stop, the ecological devastation happening every day. It is judgment.

War

"If I bring a sword on that land, and I shall say, 'Sword, go through the land,' and I shall cut off man and beast from it..." Ezekiel 14:17

This past century produced wars on the scope and scale previously unknown throughout human history. With the existence of atom and hydrogen bombs, laser-guided missiles, smart bombs, cruise missiles, biological weapons of mass destruction, and the numerous high-tech weapons not yet revealed, we are poised on the edge of eternity every day.

Satan delights to incite unjust wars wherever and whenever he can. Not all wars are simply political, domestic, or border conflict wars. Some are the judgmental application of YHWH's intervention upon the earth. Such wars will increase as the end days are biblically fulfilled.

Yea, as I walk through the valley of death,
I shall fear no evil,
For the valleys are gone and
only death awaits.
And I am the evil.
Robert Lifton from *Home From the War*

Our offspring are growing up with an understanding of "jihad," a term I never heard in my childhood. Terrorism has replaced the "war-on-drugs" and other similar issues. Gang wars are increasing and drug lords raise larger and more potent armies for their inhumane and sadistic power machines. There was a time, not too long ago, when the term "holocaust" only referred to the genocide of the Jews by the Nazis; now this term has become an everyday term and has lost some of its horrific implications.

War has become familiar to the scenes and sounds of killing, maiming, torture, genocides, and holocausts and our minds are dulled by the constant exposure to it all. Our children are introduced to video killing games at earlier ages and they become numb to the dying and many can barely discern the difference between the games and real life. The judgment called "war" is upon the whole earth.

"Happier were the victims of the sword than the victims of hunger, who pined away, stricken by the want of the fruits of the field."

Lamentations 4:9 RSV

Plague

"If I send a pestilence into the land, and I shall pour out My wrath on it in blood, to cut off man and beast,..." Ezekiel 14:19

Outbreaks of AIDS, ebola, ecoli, exotic diseases, manmade viruses, and older ones such as TB and polio are routinely paraded before our eyes in the media. Every year there is a new strain of the flu virus. New strains of biological and disease weapons are being manufactured worldwide. Science and medicine can't keep up with the requirements for new treatments for all the new ailments in the earth.

These judgmental plagues often provide opportunities for greed and exploitation to flourish. They are also opportunities for people of faith to practice compassion and availability to those with health issues. Mother Teresa gained worldwide fame and honor for her compassion upon the sick and dying of India. People of faith can intercede between "the living and the dead". They can "lay on hands," "anoint with oil," and "prayer" for healing according to scripture (see James 5:14).

"I looked and saw a pale horse. He who sat on it had the name Death, and the grave followed with him. And authority was given to them over a fourth of the earth, to kill with sword, and with hunger, and with death (plague), and by the beasts of the earth." Revelation 6:8

These judgments were not YHWH's original intention for His earth but came as the promised result of sin, disobedience, and rebellion. The intention of these judgments is not to simply punish sin but to move the hearts and minds of mankind toward their Creator. Their design is to encourage repentance and returning to the original covenant so YHWH can again bless His earth.

The Blessings of Obedience

Blessings, like judgments, are conditional. Nothing happens coincidentally with YHWH. He doesn't toss blessings or judgments around out of cosmic boredom. He always acts with reasoned purpose, cosmic and eternal, and has wisely and lovingly revealed those purposes within the sacred text of the scriptures. There are many conditions for blessings; we merely mention three of them:

Worship

"YHWH is Spirit. Those who worship Him must worship Him in spirit and in truth." John 4:24

Worship is why we were created in the first place. It is the major part of what is defined as relationship. **For a relationship to have integrity, the lessor must always honor the greater.** Everything we are and do is to be a worshipful and covenant founded relationship with YHWH. He does, however, require a worship that embraces truth (reality) and spirit (freedom of wind) or it is considered to be false worship. True worship accrues glory (kavod=weight) to YHWH, meanwhile false worship demeans, dishonors, and diminishes the brightness of His radiance.

I recall an old revivalist named A.W.Tozer referring to idolatry as "thinking thoughts about God that are unworthy of Him (see *The Pursuit of God*)."

Many times the scriptures speak of people as "seekers." YHWH promises to be found by those who are "true (truth) seekers." The scriptures also speak of YHWH being a seeker. In John 4:23, YHWH says, "He is seeking worshippers who will worship Him in spirit and in truth." It is not difficult to realize His emphasis is upon the worshipper and not the worship. In other words, He is not as concerned about the form or expression of worship as He is about the heart/mind condition of the worshipper.

Indigenous people are correct in referring to the Creator as the "Great Mystery (Spirit)." There must be mystery for the terms "awe" and "wonder" to have validity. The modern, secular society has reduced mystery to simple ignorance. Mystery becomes confined to child likeness while the adults pretend to account for everything. They believe that the doctrines of men and the traditions of religious systems have sufficiently answered all of life's questions. At least one mystery remains; how can such arrogance be justified and does mankind, in general, simply have the largest blind spot in the universe? When, Who and to what will we bow in humble reverence?

A clean, pure, and holy environment enhances all worship expressions and infuses the dance, language, songs, drums, regalia, relationships, work, family, and the living with great beauty and inestimable worth. Obedience, which is better than sacrifice, is the foundation of all such worship.

Thankfulness

*"..because, although they knew Elohim, they did not esteem Him as Elohim. Nor **gave thanks**, but became vain in their reasonings and their undiscerning heart was darkened."* Romans 1:21 (emphasis mine)

Everything we have and are is a gift from the Creator. These gifts have enough intrinsic value that Yeshua the Messiah was sent to redeem them and imbue them with eternal life. Two of these gifts are opportunity and responsibility. We have not been abandoned to find our own way in the darkness, but we possess vision, purpose, and a glorious future. **With gratitude we can embrace YHWH's trust and faith in us.**

The scriptures say that "without a vision the people perish (Proverbs 29:18)." The contrary is also true – without people the vision perishes. YHWH is inviting us to be thankful, visionary, and available to embrace our stewardship as His loving design for mankind. A great way to thank YHWH is to thank someone everyday and not ignoring even the slightest opportunities to be helpful, kind, and loving.

Stewardship

Our stewardship responsibilities are not only for our benefit. We are called to act on behalf of those who are weak, blind, deaf, and lame, physically and spiritually. We are to instruct those who are ignorant of our responsibilities. We are to disciple those unable to grasp our opportunities. We are to partner with those without understanding, experience, or wisdom. Note these significant opportunities and responsibilities:

The poor – *"Do not keep from doing what is right and fair in trying to help a poor brother when he has a problem."* Exodus 23:6

The stranger – *Do not do wrong to a stranger or make it hard for him. For you were strangers in the land of Egypt."* Exodus 22:21

The Levite – *"Do not stop caring for the Levite (ministries) who is in your town for he has no share of what is given to you."* Deut.14:27

The widows and orphans – *"Do not bring trouble to any woman whose husband has died or any child whose parents have died."* Exodus 22:22

Worship, gratitude, and stewardship are all conditions of a person's heart (thinking). Many other good things can be built upon the foundation of these three conditions. These three characterize a person's spirit, ambience, and attitude. They reveal what motivates someone. They are the true heartfelt values. **We must truly want to obey more than merely wanting the blessings of obedience.** The fact that many people experience the blessings of obedience indicates that a heart of obedience exists first.

YHWH covenanted with mankind to act in certain ways toward them. He reserves the right to intervene because He is consistent in His relationships with mankind; often such intervention is called a miracle. Many times miracles occur as proofs of the power of His presence and/or the power of His names. He can and does step outside known "laws," not breaking them but applying loftier ones in special circumstances.

Think of the laws of aerodynamics as an example – they do not break the law of gravity but apply a higher principle that allows for gravity to be overcome as long as lift, momentum, direction, and stability are maintained.

YHWH can produce miracles through mankind and overcoming the overwhelming ecological crisis mankind faces will certainly require equally overwhelming miracles.

The blessings of obedience have their source in the generous, merciful, and gracious hand of YHWH (remember the name YHWH means "The hand securing existence"). The Torah book of Leviticus, chapter 26 reveals 8 blessings from YHWH toward the land of those whose hearts and hands are obedient.

Ecological Health

"I will give you rain at the right time. So the land will give its food and the trees will give their fruit." Leviticus 26:4

George Otis Jr. writes of the transformation of a community;

"Take Almolonga, a small town of 20,000 in the highlands of Guatemala. In the early 1970's, the alcoholism rate in this dark and impoverished community had reached a staggering 99%. The entire town seemed locked in a downward spiral of superstition, corruption, and poverty. When I visited Almolonga in early November 1998, I discovered God had been at work. Upwards of 92% of the town's population is now born again (experienced YHWH's miracle of redemption)! The evidence, which may be seen at every turn includes a forest of churches and workplaces dedicated to the Lord. The results of this transformation have been nothing short of

amazing. Previously impoverished famers displayed 5 lb. beets and carrots as big as a man's arm. Before the spiritual turnaround these growers were exporting 4 truckloads of produce a month. Now they leave town forty times a week!" (The Sentinel Group Newsletter, Nov.25, 1998)

Ecological health is a blessing that YHWH is bringing through prayer-fueled visitations with reports coming in from Cali, Columbia, a community whose past reputation was known only for its drug cartel; Kiambu, Kenya, Africa; Hemet, California and others. As George Otis Jr. wrote, "The only conclusion is that something wonderful is sweeping the earth." (ibid., Sentinel Newsletter)

Economic Health

"And your threshing shall last till the time of the grape harvest, and the grape harvest shall last till the time of sowing. And you shall eat your bread until you have enough, and shall dwell in your land safely." Leviticus 26:5

Economic health remains in the hands of the Creator Who is generous of heart and kind beyond all measure. He can and does create wealth. He is able to bless economies as evidence of His promise-keeping nature. Severe economic hardships are not even hindrances to YHWH – He is able!

Citing from the Sentinel Newsletter again;

"Alcohol addiction has abated dramatically and the town's jails have been closed for lack of use. Idolatry and superstition have also fled, leaving behind a people dedicated to fervent prayer and honest labor. One farmer told me their growing time has dropped from 65 days to 25 days – with yields so robust that agricultural experts from the United States have been flocking to Almolonga to examine their farming techniques. Asked to explain this phenomenon, the farmers point to stickers affixed to the windshield and mud flaps of their shiny, new Mercedes trucks. The messages are simple and straightforward: "The gift of God," "Go Forward in Faith," and "God is my Stronghold."

YHWH hasn't chosen Almolonga out of respect for those people alone; He would choose every place where humility, repentance, and obedience are practiced.

The land (dirt) is able to produce far more than what is considered "normal," but it can't when the defilements of disobedience are on it. The blessings of obedience for economic health wait upon us and our actions.

"For ground that is drinking the rain often falling on it, and is bearing plants fit for those by whom it is tilled, receives the blessing of Elohim." Hebrews 6:7

Personal Security

"And I shall give peace (shalom) in the land, and you shall lie down and no one make you afraid. And I shall clear the land of evil beasts, and not let the sword go through your land." Leviticus 26:6

Mankind is functioning out fear more than any other motivation. Decisions are being made based on the fears of both the known and unknown.

King George, in the year he would die of cancer, addresses the Keeper at the Gate of the Year, "Give me a light so I can face the unknown." The Keeper wisely replied, "Put your hand in the hand of God. It will be for you brighter than a light and safer than the known." (a taped message by Ravi Zacharias)

Yeshua plainly told us that in these days *"men's hearts would fail them for fear of what's coming on the earth* (Luke 21:26)."

Personal security is a subject important to everyone as an increase in violence, murder, home-invasion, rape, drug and gang violence, and war occurs. Political and economic instability produce other kinds of fear.

Mankind yearns for outward and inward security. It is a security that is more than the electronic and surveillance systems can provide. The security longed for is provided by the knowledge of YHWH's protection in circumstances where fear would normally prevail. This blessing is allowing the *"peace of YHWH to rule and reign in your hearts."*

Read this account of personal security:

(This account was sent by e-mail from Richard Black and happened around December 18th, 1998. It is condensed for the sake of space.)

"Ken, Britt, and I were all awake at 4 a.m. and were led to pray for various things. Now to the events which we were being prepared for in advance. It was about 10 a.m. and we had been to see a waterfall which was a tourist attraction outside the town near us (there were 7 persons in all). Just as Ken unlocked the passenger side of the Pajero for Jeff to get in, we all heard a noise in the bush on the uphill side of the road. A single man with an AK-47 military rifle came out of the bush yelling things in French and loading his gun. He fired a shot into the air clueing us to the fact that he was bent on robbery. The next thing I heard was a gunshot and the barrel was pointed right at my chest. I felt the air and looked down to see the hole I thought would be there, but nothing hit me. I remember Ken specifically binding Satan in the situation.

(The robber shot one of the women in the back. Another robber joined in and they began gathering up the items they wanted to steal. Believing these robbers were shooting blank cartridges, the missionaries went after the robbers to retrieve their goods. After overpowering them, they left the scene.)

At the top of the hill, I took the clip out of the gun to make sure there weren't any blanks in the chamber and was met with a realization that still has me a little shaken, and completely in awe of the power of God Almighty. The man was using real bullets! I even racked out the one that was ready to be fired and it was a real, life-sized AK-47 bullet with the power to kill. During the course of the event our God made six bullets disappear into thin air. God intervened in a way that has increased all our faith and given us cause to testify to the mighty power of our awesome God!" Karl

When YHWH doesn't provide personal security, it doesn't indicate some personal sin is present or that He dislikes the individuals. He is YHWH and retains the right to operate the "keys of death" over all individuals. For some people, it is time to stay and fulfill some mission, for others it is time to come home and be with YHWH. He decides these things.

Malachi 3:17 "....And I shall spare them as a man spares his own son who serves him." Mankind is attempting to spare himself by hiding and hoarding, but YHWH is the only source of security for mankind.

Civil Security

"And you shall pursue your enemies, and they shall fall by the sword before you." Leviticus 26:7

I don't believe our recent military adventures have been successful simply because we have out-gunned the opposition. We may actually be sowing a seed the reaping of which we may later regret. Our fragile political, financial, and spiritual support of Israel has kept us in YHWH's grace. This support of Israel is waning and we find ourselves at an historical crossroads. Our support of the division of Israel with a Palestinian State will bring YHWH's judgment upon us in a massive way (See Joel 3:2). Reaping is never eliminated, it often is postponed until another time.

Those who follow the good road and are obedient to the commands of Yeshua must begin to soften their hearts and begin "turning their swords into plowshears and spears into farming tools (see Is.2:4)."

One day there will be total civil security and that will be when the King of the Universe rules this unruly world.

International Security

"And five of you shall pursue a hundred, and a hundred of you pursue ten thousand. And your enemies shall fall by the sword before you."

Leviticus 26:8

I believe the disciples of Yeshua can apply this verse for spiritual warfare. The presence and power of the Ruach HaKodash (Holy Spirit) multiplies, exponentially, our efforts and our effectiveness. When people are obedient, great power is unleashed for them and to them.

Remember YHWH does not endorse unjust wars. There are no scriptures that grant the rights to kill others simply because they don't accept democracy or someone's definition of freedom. The only scriptural right to kill anyone seems to be against those who are disobedient. Israel appears to be the only nation that was founded upon the obedience versus disobedience principle. They are to be an example for the rest of the world.

Honor and Growth

"And I shall turn to you and make you bear fruit, and shall increase you, and shall establish My covenant with you." Leviticus 26:9

How sad and meager have been many of our fleshly efforts at promoting Kingdom growth, when YHWH would have generously provided it. YHWH is holding back blessing but eagerly waits to release it at every opportunity. YHWH wants, greatly desires, and yearns tenderly for us to bear lasting and much fruit for His Kingdom. Note He promises to "turn" to us and secures His promise in His covenant-keeping power. What a generous and great Yah we serve!

Recall the grafting process revealed in Roman 11. The purpose was not merely to bring Jews and Gentiles together, although that is a powerful incentive, but more importantly to double the harvest. Maybe we should increase our horizons to include the ideas and principles of a double harvest.

Creativity

"And you shall eat the old supply, and clear out the old because of the new." Leviticus 26:10

YHWH creates new mercies every morning, not serving up yesterday's left-overs nor borrowing from tomorrow's supply. He is able to inspire great and awesome creative ideas in His people. He wants us to become redemptively creative in these last days. He will inspire many inventions, introduce many cures, and present many solutions to significant problems.

Many of these things will come in dreams and visions beyond the rational contemplations of mankind. These Divinely inspired creativities will not only solve problems, but will create wealth for the Kingdom of YHWH. **YHWH loves us, He likes us, and He is not poor!** He delights to inspire and illumine in order that results in creative designs for His world are utilized.

Habitation not Visitation

"And I shall set My Dwelling Place (Succah) in your midst, and My being shall not reject you. And I shall walk in your midst, and shall be you Elohim, and you shall be My people." Leviticus 26:11-12

YHWH has been working throughout history in every generation to restore the relationship He had with Adam and Eve in the Garden of Eden. He yearns to walk with us again in the "cool of the evening (the Ruach HaKodesh)."

Through the death and resurrection of Yeshua the Messiah, reconciliation restores a wide open door for such fellowship. Through obedient stewardship we can make a home for YHWH.

Do we understand what makes the land sick? What defiles the land? How can we act with humility and repentance making a habitation for YHWH?

The next chapter explores these questions and provides some answers for our consideration.

The blessings of obedience are huge in the scope and scheme of life. We ought to receive them in their fullness. They provide wonderful and powerful motivations accompanied with confidence and peace, integrity and purpose, a future and a hope. We are so blessed!

HERE
WERE HANGED
38
SIOUX INDIANS
DEC. 26TH 1862.

Chapter Two

What Defiles the Land?

"For the intense longing of the creation eagerly waits for the revealing of the sons of Elohim.

For the creation was subjected to futility, not by choice, but because of Him who subjected it, in anticipation, that the creation itself also shall be delivered from the bondage to corruption into the esteemed freedom of the children of Elohim.

For we know that all creation groans together, and suffers the pains of childbirth together until now." Romans 8:19-22

Sin, trespass, disobedience and iniquity defile the land. It is obvious from scripture that the land suffers because of our sins.

"I will lay waste the land, because they have not been faithful," says Adonai YHWH." Ezekiel 15:8

To not be "faithful" is expressed by the Hebrew word *ma'al* which means to *trespass*. This is to cover up, to act secretly or treacherously and is written as *iniquity* in many places in scripture.

"...the land which you are going to possess is a land unclean through the uncleanness of the peoples of the land, by their abominations with which they have filled it, from one end to another, by their uncleanness." Ezra 9:11

YHWH sees the land as defiled and unclean because of sin and abomination. The scriptures reveal four specific sins that defile the land.

In North America we have defilements in two different contexts; defilements that preceeded contact with Europeans, referred to as *ancient defilements*, and subsequent post-contact defilements referred to as *contemporary defilements.* Both defilements require humility and repentance for healing of the land to occur. The Ruach HaKodesh (Holy Spirit) is the only true Agent of Conviction (cf. John 16:8) and He will reveal where humility and repentance are required.

These defilements are listed as; idolatry, sexual immorality, bloodshed, and broken treaties (covenants).

Ancient and Contemporary Defilements

First Nations peoples need to be aware of *ancient defilements* and be repentant for them. However, you ask, "Should I repent for sins others have committed?" Good question.

In both the books of Ezra and Nehemiah, the leaders of Israel repented for the sins of their forefathers so that Jerusalem could again be built and might prosper.

The scriptures speak of sins following us to the 3rd and 4th generations except for illegitimacy which defiles to the 10th generation (cf. Deuteronomy 5:9 and 23:2). We must be repentant for past generations if only to break the cycle of harmful and defiling affects upon the land and its people, especially where shamanism, animism, and some kinds of totemisms have occurred.

We can all relate to the *contemporary defilements* as we observe and participate in the sins of the present generation. Here, humble and repentant, believers can act as intercessors for those unwilling to repent. YHWH will help us heal the land because He tells us that *"He resists the proud but gives grace to the humble* (cf.1 Peter 5:5)."

have you seen ATHENA?

IN NASHVILLE, TN -

Here are the four land defiling sins:

Idolatry

"And first I shall repay double for their crookedness and their sin, because they have defiled My land with the dead bodies of their disgusting idols, and have filled My inheritance with their abominations." Jeremiah 16:18

This passage is incisive about YHWH's hatred for idolatry and its defiling of the land. Note the issues mentioned here; He repays double for idolatry; they defiled His land; He hates idolatry and finds it disgusting; they filled the land with idolatry; they defiled His inheritance.

What is idolatry?

"An idol or image is a controllable representation of our best loyalties and visions, an effort to reduce to manageable and predictable forms the sources of value and power in our lives."

(Walter Bruggermann, *The Land:Overtures to Biblical Theology,*Philadelphia;Fortress Press,1977,pg.4-5)

A.W.Tozer in his best-selling book *The Pursuit of God* states that "idolatry is thinking thoughts about God that are unworthy of Him."

Idolatry begins in the heart (mind) as rejection of the truths already known about YHWH and proceeds to various manifestations of the thought life expressed as worship, i.e. carved objects, power ideas, position, wealth, etc. Even the traditions of men can become idols as the Ruach HaKodesh (Holy Spirit) attempts to introduce new expressions or thoughts into our worship forms and systems.

A.W. Tozer said, "If a man were to tell me what comes into his mind when asked the question, 'What comes to your mind when you think about God?' I could accurately predict the future of that man." (see *The Pursuit of God*). He went on to say the same thing about churches and religious movements. Our thoughts about YHWH will determine the integrity of our worship and what our worship expressions are or will become.

The scriptures make obvious YHWH's hatred of idolatry and we understand that, what we have ignored is the fact that idolatry defiles the land.

Our communities, our celebrations, and our ceremonies are filled with various expressions of idolatry, ancient and contemporary. We live under the curse (Ancient Hebrew word is aleph-lamed-hey, *alah*) which idolatry brings upon the land and its inhabitants.

"Their idols are silver and gold, the work of men's hands. They have mouths, but they do not speak; they have eyes, but they do not see; they have ears, but they do not hear; they have noses, but they do not smell; they have hands, but they do not handle; they have feet, but they do not walk; they make no sound through their throat. The ones who make them, shall become like them. All who trust in them." Psalm 115:4-8

Here is a warning and a curse spoken by YHWH about idolaters. He says they will become like whatever it is they are worshipping. Moreover their mouths won't speak the truth, their eyes won't see clearly, their ears won't hear His voice, their noses won't smell the stench of sin, their hands won't do His work, and their feet will not walk the path of obedience. What a terrible way to live!

"And it came to be, through her (Israel) frivolous whoring, that she defiled the land and committed adultery with stones and wood." Jeremiah 3:9

"YHWH is Sovereign forever and ever; those who worship false gods will be taken from the land." Psalm 10:16 New Life Bible

We believe the land is looking and listening for the sounds of true worship. It is longing for clear and clean praise for YHWH. It is joining in wherever it occurs. Many of the bird and whale songs are actually Hebrew notes for YHWH's names. Creation is waiting on us. Personally, I want to be the kind of believer that heals the land by true worship and praise of my Creator Who is worthy of all expressions of worship.

All sounds, songs, movements, and instruments can be redeemed and their expressions directed toward YHWH as praise. The dance, drama, art, language, regalia, and music can be used to express the truths of our heart's love for YHWH.

For many years worship expressions in the West were largely mono-cultural, Euro. The indigenous sounds, instruments, drums, and dances were considered unredeemable to the "Christian" culture. It was demanded of indigenous people to leave their sin-stained culture and join the sin-stained culture of the Euros'. We have been deprived of so much worship, the beauty and power of which has been recently restored to indigenous people, even over the strong objections to many Euro-centric systems. As we often say to people, "YHWH looks on the heart of the drummer, not the drum itself."

We need to overthrow the idolatry of our own preferences and allow Yah's people to worship Him in the manner and with the expressions He gave them.

Immorality

"Do not lie with a male as with a woman, it is an abomination. And do not have intercourse with any beast, to defile yourself with it. And a woman, does stand before a beast to mate with it, it is a perversion. Do not defile yourselves with all these, for by all these the nations are defiled, which I am driving out before you. Thus the land became defiled, therefore I punished it for its crookedness, and the land vomited out its inhabitants. But you, you shall guard My instructions (torah) and My right-rulings, and not do any of these abominations, the native nor stranger who sojourns among you, because the men of the land who were before you have done all these abominations, and thus the land became defiled, so let not the vomit you out for defiling it, as it vomited out the nations that were before you."

Leviticus 18:22-28

Sexual immorality includes fornication, adultery, rape, incest, bestiality, homosexuality, pornography, prostitution, lying, stealing, disloyalty, and promiscuity. These all produce major strongholds not easily broken.

"Do not profane your daughter by making her a whore, so that the land does not whore, and the land becomes filled with wickedness."

Leviticus 19:29

A veteran porn star says, "I think about getting a normal job, going to school, but people would say, "Aren't you....?" Every day I want to be a schoolteacher, but I can just imagine the parents saying that I can't be around their kids."

Besides a child and a sister, this woman has parents, a Sunday school teacher, a former pastor, and others who love and pray for her. All of them grieve for her. So does the land.

"For since the creation of the world His invisible qualities have been clearly seen, being understood from what has been made, both His everlasting power and Mightiness, for them to be without excuse, because, although they knew Elohim, they did not esteem Him as Elohim, nor gave thanks, but became vain in their reasonings, and their undiscerning heart was darkened. Claiming to be wise, they became fools, and changed the esteem of the incorruptible Elohim into the likeness of an image of corruptible man, and of birds and four-footed beasts and of reptiles. Therefore Elohim gave them up to uncleanness in the lust of their hearts, to disrespect their bodies among themselves, who changed the truth of Elohim into the falsehood, and worshipped and served what was created rather than the Creator, who is blessed forever. Amen. Because of this Elohim gave them over to degrading passions. For even their women exchanged natural relations for what is against nature, and likewise, the men also, having left natural relations with women, burned in their lust for one another, men with men committing indecency, and receiving back the reward which was due for their straying. And even as they did not think it worthwhile to possess the knowledge of Elohim, Elohim gave them over to a worthless mind, to do what is improper."
Romans 1:21-27

Several years ago I asked a group of high school students to write down two things; what sexual sins they had committed against the opposite sex, and what sexual sins had been committed against them by the opposite gender. I took their anonymous confessions and formed them into the following prayer of reconciliation. For three hours these young people wept and repented for their sins. What a wonderful healing took place in their lives and upon their land. I've included that prayer here to be prayed with humility and with a spirit of repentance. We suggest readers pray the following: (not all will apply personally, but take home to heart all that do).

"My heavenly Father, Creator of the human body and spirit, I know I am a sinner and have sinned against You. I have sinned against others, including my father, mother, brothers, sisters, and friends.

I have abused them physically and touched them inappropriately. I have lusted for their bodies and ignored their feelings and heartfelt values. I have treated them like garbage and put them down to their faces and behind their backs. Some I have cursed, lied to, made false accusations against them, and flirted with them with no intention of demonstrating any real interest in them. I used them to get my own way and to enjoy their bodies for my own pleasure as if they belonged to me. I have slapped, hit, and punched them in anger or to get my own way. I have verbally and sexually abused them, treating them as inferior. I rejected them through indifference and unwillingness to show compassion. I have broken promises and forced them to reveal secrets about themselves or others which I have used against them when convenient. I have joked, crudely, about their bodies, gender, weight, appearance, or color without shame or remorse.

I have considered them to be objects I can use and throw away. I have viewed pornography with evil intentions and wicked imaginations. I have made racial remarks-being rude, mean-spirited, starting gossip or rumors about them. I have cursed them by encouraging them to sin with me or for me, without regard to their parents, siblings, peers, church, or Yeshua. I have misjudged them, using them to make myself appear bigger or better. I have been a terrible example and have harmed my own body with drugs, alcohol, and other substances, jeopardizing the health of my future and my future offspring. I have been argumentative and unforgiving.

Knowing my own heart and mind, and not knowing all, there is much more I could and should confess. Heavenly Father, I ask Your forgiveness and I will ask those I have sinned against for their forgiveness. Father, I ask You to heal all the hurts I have done to others. I ask the blood of Yeshua to cleanse my heart, mind, and memories. I ask You to bring freedom to those I harmed and to those who may have harmed me.

I renounce all areas in which satan has taken ground in my life because of my actions, attitudes, and motivations. Adonai, I ask You to give this ground back to me so I may build pure, proper, and holy relationships with these special people You created. Please help me, Ruach HaKodesh to be sincerely loving to all people.

Because only free people can set others free, please free men/women to see others the way You see them. Father, by Your grace, they are deserving of Your love, mercy, respect, dignity, and joy. Help me to see Yeshua in them and to know they are servants even as I am. In the name of Adonai Yeshua HaMeshiach of Nazareth I pray. Amen!"

If you've never committed some of these sins, it is proper to intercede for those who have. If the Ruach HaKodesh convicted you of any, please respond in humility and with repentance before Him. If restitution toward others is required, do not hesitate to make things right with them.

"Do not speak of guarding a clean earth with a dirty heart....Do not ask for the blessing of heaven when you have every intentions of living like hell. Get the ground of your life broken up, watered in tears, sown in righteousness. Become a man or woman God can trust with the care of His creation." (Ibid., Pratney, p.170)

We are aware our world is paying a bitter price for our defilement of the land through immorality. There is disease, suffering, suicide, domestic violence, anger, hatred, perversion, vengeance, and broken relationships, all because of defilement. We need a sweeping renewal of holiness throughout our world, and we must make a commitment to repent and "lay the axe to the root" of our defilements. Compromise with immorality will only produce continuing moral, social, spiritual, and land hardships.

Burial of the Dead
at the Battle of Wounded Knee S.D.
NorthWestern Photo Co
Chadron Neb

Sometimes fasting and prayer can help people with the hurts of past sins, and sins committed against them. There is healing in spending more time before Adonai and His torah (word) in the area of moral and sexual purity. It is a blessing to see the strong emphasis amongst our youth for sexual abstinence until marriage! They and the land will be blessed by such commitments and righteous living.

This humility and repentance releases upon the earth an anointing of righteousness and holiness. It also releases the fear of Adonai. It is a powerful tool in the hands of Ruach HaKodesh to bring conviction upon a people group or nation. Let's become super-diligent in the area of repenting for immorality.

Bloodshed

"And do not profane the land where you are, for blood profanes the land, and the land is not pardoned for the blood that is shed on it, except by the blood of him who shed it." Numbers 35:33

Bloodshed includes murder, unjust warfare, suicide, infanticide, abortion, and some accidental deaths.

Remember the account of Cain killing (crushing the head) his brother Abel:

"And He (Elohim) said, "What have you done? The voice of your brother's blood cries out to me from the ground. And now you are cursed from the earth, which has opened its mouth to receive your brother's blood from your hand." Genesis 4:10-11

The word "cries" means to shriek or shout out in a sense of danger. Truly the ground was suffering because of this terrible defilement. Why? Because the earth was made to provide and produce life and here was compelling evidence and the presence of death. The ground itself felt the pressure of impending judgment for which it had no advocate except to cry out to its Creator for help and justice.

"That on you should come all the righteous blood shed on the earth, from the blood of righteous Abel to the blood of Zacharias son of Barachias, whom you murdered between the Dwelling Place and the altar."

Matthew 23:35 (this is about 14 generations)

"And they shed innocent blood, the blood of their sons and daughters, whom they offered to the idols of Canaan; and the land was defiled with blood." Psalm 106:38

The scriptures present many accounts of bloodshed, including murder, war, infanticide, abortion, and suicide. The Psalmist David was prevented from building the Temple because he was a "man of violence (war)." YHWH didn't want aspects of bloodshed to become the principle barrier to worship in His Temple.

Many non-biblical nations have experienced a history of bloodshed and the earth is covered with defiled ground because of it. Our own continent has evidence of bloodshed defilements of the ancient kind.

Carl Waldman, writing in the *Atlas of the North American Indian* about the Toltecs (Aztecs) said, "Tradition has it that the peaceful Topiltzin-Quetzalcoatl fell out of power when he tried to ban human sacrifice, which the Toltecs practiced on a large scale. As a result, his followers- that is, the followers of the benign Plumed Serpent- were overthrown by devotees of the god Tezcatlipoca, deity of the night (pg.11-12)."

"For look, YHWH is coming out of His place to punish the inhabitants of the earth for their crookedness. And the earth shall disclose her blood, and no longer cover her slain (dead)." Isaiah 26:21

Look at these statistics of recent bloodshed:

-massacre at Littleton, Colorado in Columbine High School, 1999 -15 dead

-massacre at Virginia Tech College – 33 dead

-massacre at Red lake Indian Reservation, Minnesota – 10 dead

-massacre and movie theater Aurora, Colorado – 12 dead

-massacre at Sandy Hook Elementary School, Newtown, Connecticut – 26 dead

INDIAN LAND FOR SALE

GET A HOME

OF

YOUR OWN

EASY PAYMENTS

PERFECT TITLE

POSSESSION

WITHIN

THIRTY DAYS

FINE LANDS IN THE WEST

IRRIGATED
IRRIGABLE

GRAZING

AGRICULTURAL
DRY FARMING

-hundreds of thousands in Kosovo and Serbia war, 1998-1999
-1-1.5 million of Rwanda since 1995
-2-3 million in Cambodia in the reign of Pol Pot
-6 million Jews in the holocaust
-22 million soldiers and civilians in World War II
- 100's of thousands since 9/11 2001 in the war on terror
-29 million First Nations people of North America from "discovery" until 1899 – thousands more since
-45 million infants in abortion in North America since 1972

In the same amount of time in which we killed our infants, 2 million Americans, of all ages, died in automobile accidents. This means an American infant has an 18 times greater chance of being killed on purpose in a mother's womb than in an accident on a highway. **The most dangerous place for an American baby is in its mother's womb.** How sad! How defiling!

Wherever bloodshed has occurred, blood cries out to the Creator for justice to be done. He is a Just YHWH, committed to making things right in the earth. We praise Him for His great mercy and long-suffering to us.

The Body of Messiah must prepare for the end-time scenario that includes massive bloodshed (1/3 of all living things –cf. Rev.9:18). Healing the land intercessors will have to be raised up in huge numbers.

Additional scriptures: Deuteronomy 21:1-9;22-23; 22:8; Acts 15:17-29; Matthew 23:34-36

Broken Treaties (Covenants)

"See, YHWH is making the earth empty and making it waste, and shall overturn its surface, and shall scatter abroad its inhabitants. The earth is completely emptied and utterly plundered, for YHWH has spoken this word. The earth shall mourn and wither, the world shall languish and wither, the haughty people of the earth shall languish. For the earth has been defiled under its inhabitants, because they have transgressed the Torot, changed the

law, broken to the everlasting treaty (covenant). Therefore a curse shall consume the earth, and those who dwell in it be punished. Therefore the inhabitants of the earth shall be burned, and few men shall be left (a remnant)." Isaiah 24:1, 3-6

Broken treaties include treaties between tribes and nations, divorce, certain bankruptcies, church splits, etc. A broken treaty may indicate an evil intention in making the treaty in the first place. In other words, some treaties were made with no intention of fulfilling them. It is evil and defiles the land.

The history of treaties between the First Nations in North America and the governments of the United States and Canada is large and dismal. The first treaty was a verbal agreement with the Pilgrims in Plymouth, MA that the land would not be stolen from the original inhabitants but a "just and fair" price would be paid for the land. This verbal agreement lasted only fifty years. The first written treaty was made in 1778 and at least 370 documented treaties were signed over the next 100 years. All of them were broken by the U.S. Government.

"The utmost good faith shall <u>always</u> be observed toward the Indians; their land and property shall <u>never</u> be taken from them without their consent; and their property, rights and liberty, they shall <u>never</u> be invaded or disturbed, unless in just and lawful wars authorized by Congress; but laws founded on justice and humanity shall from time to time be made, <u>for preventing wrongs</u> done to them, and for preserving peace and friendship with them." U.S. Congress 1787 (emphasis mine)

This treaty was enforced for 3 months and then broken.

Most of the treaty breaking resulted in bloodshed. In 1800 there were 260,000 natives in California; by 1900 only 20,000 had survived. By 1899, in all of North America, there were only 237,000 surviving First Nations people.

The original American colonies paid bounties for native extermination - $130 for men and half that for women and children. Great Britain offered 40 pounds for male scalps and 20 for female and children's scalps. Once a treaty was broken, it appears the freedom for bloodshed was unleashed and the land defiled.

In 1990 the Native American Graves Protection and Repatriation Act was passed to redress centuries of injustice by allowing native tribes to reclaim human remains, funery and sacred objects, and items of cultural importance stolen from native grave sites. According to estimates by the Congressional Budget Office, the federally funded agencies and museums possess up to 15 million cultural artifacts and 200,000 First Nation human remains. As of 2000, only 512 sacred objects and 9,700 human remains had been returned to native tribes. **In what other context would the intentional foot-dragging of fulfilling an act of Congress be tolerated?**

This foot-dragging is tolerated because it involves money, politics, racism, lobbying by museums and archeologists, and the deliberate breaking of an official treaty. It is defiling the land!

The treaties concerning the education and health care for First Nations people continues to be most reluctantly fulfilled and every obstacle possible is put in the way of receiving the promises of the treaty. President George W. Bush (his 1st act as President), unilaterally, cut the B.I.A. (Bureau of Indian Affairs) health budget by 20%, without Congressional authorization. This one executive directive put large portions of the native population at health risk, especially the elders. It broke another treaty.

Because sowing and reaping is true, America faces a dark and dreadful future.

"Elohim said, "If a man puts away (divorces) his wife, and she goes from him and becomes another man's, does he return to her again? Would not that land be made greatly unclean?.." Jeremiah 3:1

It isn't difficult to understand the defilement of divorce but it often goes unrecognized that the land is defiled by it. People who have experienced the trauma and heartbreak of divorce should cleanse their property through repentance (teshuva), possible reconciliation, and heartfelt prayers.

Some bankruptcies are due to unforeseen economic conditions, questionable decision-making processes, or just outright mismanagement. Some may be due to extreme health issues, etc. Therefore, not every bankruptcy can be labeled as "treaty breaking." Each case has to be understood in its context. If you have experienced bankruptcy, you need not carry guilt – make good, wise, and just decision for a fresh start. If your bankruptcy was the result of covert activity, assets being hidden, accounts being juggled, etc. treaty breaking has occurred and the land defiled. Things should be made right with creditors and repentance made.

Be careful when making personal treaties (agreements) that your word is fulfilled. Treaties don't just affect us, they also affect the land.

Summary

I saw God wash

the world last night.

Ah, would He had washed me.

William Stidger

These defilements of the land are real because they are caused by real sin, disobedience, and rebellion against YHWH's Torah (Word). Sin is not simply the breaking of moral codes or YHWH's instructions, but it carries the viruses of pain, terror, and defilement with it. Even the final judgments include and important warning for those intent on harming the earth:

"And the nations were enraged, and Your wrath has come, and the time of the dead to be judged, and to give the reward to Your servants the prophets and to the set-apart ones, and to those who fear Your name, small and great, and to destroy those who destroy the earth." Revelation 11:18

Satan's work is about destroying the earth through defilements. Read what YHWH says about satan:

"How you have fallen from the heavens, o Helel, son of the morning! You have been cut down to the ground, you who laid low the gentiles! For you have said in your heart, 'Let me go up to the heavens, let me raise my throne above the stars of El, and let me sit in the mount of meeting on the sides of the north; let me go up above the heights of the clouds, let me be like the

Most High.' But you are brought down to the grave, to the sides of the Pit. Those who stare at you, and ponder over you, saying, 'Is this the man who made the earth tremble, who shook reigns, who made the world as a wilderness and destroyed its cities, who would not open the house of his prisoners?' All the sovereigns of the gentiles, all of them, were laid in esteem, everyone in his own house; but you have been thrown from your grave like an abominable branch, like the garment of those who are slain, thrust through with a sword, who go down to the stones of the pit, like a trampled corpse. You are not joined with them in burial, for <u>you have destroyed your</u> <u>land</u> and slain your people. Let the seed of evil-doers never be mentioned."

Isaiah 14:12-20 (emphasis mine)

These defilements have a satanic agenda driving them with a relentless pressure increasing as the end-times approach for he "knows his time is short."

The importance and necessity of humility and repentance (teshuva) cannot be over emphasized. Our window of opportunity shrinks every day.

"We have willingly caused what Martin Buber called " a wound in the order of being, and healing that wound in our planet's being and in our own requires repentance. Indeed, any "terror" we feel at the threat of our own self-destruction without accompanying repentance is but a further expression of human arrogance." (ibid., Pratney, p.154)

What should we do?

The following chapters address the prayers of repentance, the change of thinking, the work of spiritual mapping, and the powerful act of speaking to the earth.

"The end (goal) of God's creating the world was to prepare a kingdom for His Son." Jonathon Edwards

"..the whole land has been laid waste, because no one cares."

Jeremiah 12:11 New Life

Ask yourself, *"Do I care?"*

Because YHWH made good dirt (land), our desire should be to present good dirt back to Him as our gift of stewardship.

Mt. Illiuma, AK

Chapter Three

Speak to the Earth

Remember, we are repenting for sins, rebellions, and defilements, both ancient and contemporary, over a land that is mourning. Why would land mourn?

Is it possible we have polluted the land beyond our littering, chemical intrusions, or by our neglect in stewardship of protecting water, land, and air? Is it possible that our sin has polluted the land to the extent of making it sick and sorrowful?

"YHWH said, 'What have you done? The voice of your brother's blood is crying to Me from the ground." Genesis 4:10

This account is not some sort of Divine poetic expression given in such a way as to make us feel sorry for Cain and Abel. Something lasting and real occurred that murderous day, on that ground, with that defilement of bloodshed. YHWH can hear our blood as it courses through our veins and He can hear Abel's blood as it courses through the veins of the earth.

The Hebrew word for "polluted" is *chaneph.* It means "straying from YHWH's path." No wonder the land is defiled when we sin. Pollution and sin have the same connotations and, thus, similar effects are experienced upon the land as the effects of people's sin. The land, through pollution, strays from YHWH's original intention (producing abundantly) and begins to "cry out" to its Creator for a Divine solution. Listen to the sound of these scriptures:

"How long will the land be filled with sorrow?" Jeremiah 12:4a

"It (the land) has been laid waste. Destroyed and empty, it cries with sorrow before Me. The whole land has been laid waste, because no one cares." Jeremiah 12:11

"For the land is full of people who are not faithful. Because of the bad things that have come upon it, the land is filled with sorrow, and the fields of the desert have dried up." Jeremiah 23:10

"Then Adonai will be jealous for His land and have pity on His people." Joel 2:18

What is happening here?

Does the earth cry in pain in a literal sense but with a frequency that is beyond human hearing, heard only by supernatural means? Is the earth mourning the sins of mankind and weeping over our sin and its effects upon the earth. Is the earth crying out more than believers? That's what the scriptures are saying!

"For the intense longing (literally "anxiously looking with outstretched head") of the creation eagerly waits for the revealing of the Sons of Elohim. For the creation was subjected to futility, not from choice, but because of Him who subjected it, in anticipation that the creation itself also shall be delivered (redeemed) from the bondage to corruption into the esteemed (glorious) freedom of the children of Elohim. For we know that all creation groans together, and suffers the pains of childbirth together until now. And not only so, but even we ourselves who have the first-fruits of Ruach haKodesh (the Spirit)." Romans 8:19-23a

The Sitka spruce trees of the Kenai Peninsula in Alaska suffered a devastating outbreak of the Japanese beetle. The direct cause was pollution. When the air pollution reaches a certain percentage, the spruce trees emit a frequency that is beyond human hearing but actually awakens the larvae of the Japanese beetle. They mature, eat the lining of the bark, and the spruce tree dies. The frequency they emit is similar to a high decibel shriek, so say the scientists who studied the outbreak.

We are aware that the "wages of sin is death (Romans 6:23)" but we haven't realized that such a death might extend to the very ground upon which we live, work, and worship.

The Hebrew word for "cry" is *za'aq* which means to "shriek from anguish or a sense of danger." The earth is sending out a cosmic distress signal that it is time for judgment unless and until the sinners humble themselves, pray, repent, turn from wickedness, and see YHWH "heal their land."

Speaking to the Earth

After we've accepted our responsibility as stewards of the land; after we've repented then what? After all the soul searching, regrets, and genuine attempts at reconciliation and restoration are done, then what?

A significant positive activity for the land is simply speaking to the earth. It is praying and singing over the land. It's complimenting the earth for its awesome provision for us. It is being grateful. Here are some biblical examples:

With Music

"David and the captains of the army set apart for the work some of the sons of Asaph, of Harman and of Jeduthun. They were to speak YHWH's word while and drums were playing." 1 Chronicles 25:1

"Then you will come to the hill of YHWH where there are Philistine soldiers. When you come there to the city, you will meet a group of men who speak for YHWH coming down from a high place. They will have music boxes of strings, an object to beat sounds of joy (drum), and a horn (shofar). And they will be speaking YHWH's Word." 1 Samuel 10:5

With Handclapping

"So speak My name, son of man, and clap your hands together." Ezekiel 21:14a

"For with joy you go out, and with peace you are brought in – the mountains and the hills break forth into singing before you, and all the trees of the field clap their hands." Isaiah 55:12

"The Adonai Elohim says, 'Clap your hands, stomp your feet, and say….." Ezekiel 6:11a

While Shaving

"As for you, son of man, take a sword. Use it to cut the hair from your head and face. Then weigh and divide the hair." Ezekiel 5:1

Lying Down

"Then lie on your left side. I have set the number of days for you which is the same as the number of years of their sin, 390 days. When you have completed these, you must lie down a second time, but on your right side (for 40 days)." Ezekiel 4:4-6

To Bones

"He said to me, "Speak in My name over these bones. Say to them, 'O dry bones, hear the Word of YHWH." Ezekiel 37:4

To the Wind

"Then He said to me, 'Speak to the breath (wind) in My name, son of man. Tell the breath, 'The Adonai Elohim says, 'Come forth from the four

winds, O breath, and breathe on these dead bodies to make them come to life." Ezekiel 37:9

In Warfare

"Son of man, look toward the god of the land of Magog, the leader of Rosh, Meshech, and Tubal, and speak against him."

Ezekiel 38:2

In Dreams and Visions

"In the last days I will send My Ruach HaKodesh (Spirit) on all men. Then your sons and daughters will speak YHWH's Word. Your old men will dream dreams. Your young men will see special dreams (visions). Yes, on My servants (stewards), both men and women, I will pour out My Ruach HaKodesh (Spirit) in those days." Joel 2:28-29

The scriptures have many references of actions over the land; Moses stretching his staff over the Red Sea and it parted; a king striking the ground with his arrows; the man who tore his coat into 12 pieces; Captain Naaman dipping 7 times in the Jordan; and of many that Yeshua did while on earth.

Sometimes you may have to speak to the earth over the land where you live, work, and worship. Here are some biblical examples of people who did that:

"I will cry with a loud voice for the mountains, I will cry out in sorrow for the fields, because they are laid waste. No one passes through them. The sound of cattle is not heard. The birds of the sky and the wild animals have run away." Jeremiah 9:10

"And you, son of man, prophesy to the mountains of Israel, and say, 'O mountains of Israel, hear the word of Adonai Elohim! Thus says Adonai Elohim

to the mountains, the hills, the rivers, the valleys, the desolate wastes, and the cities that have been forsaken, which become plunder and mockery to the rest of the nations around. Therefore prophesy concerning the land of Israel, and say to the mountains, the hills, the rivers, and the valleys, 'Thus says Adonai Elohim: "Behold I have spoken in My jealousy and My fury, because you have borne the shame of the nations. But you, O mountains of Israel, you shall shoot forth your branches and yield your fruit to My people Israel, for they are about to come." Ezekiel 36:1, 4, 6, 8

Here is a biblical admonition to speak to the earth in the same way one would speak to another person. YHWH is telling us the earth will be responsive to our obedience. Yeshua did this several times while with His disciples:

"Then Yeshua got up and spoke words to the wind and the high seas. The wind stopped blowing and there were no more waves. He said to them, 'Where is your faith?' The followers were surprised and afraid. They said to each other, 'What kind of man is He? He speaks to the wind and the waves and they obey Him.'" Luke 8:24-25

A little background on this account from Hebrew roots: Yeshua was speaking to a "sier" or fierce storm. The root of that word, "sier" is found in the name Esau who had proclaimed his purpose to "kill his brother Jacob when their father had died (cf. Genesis 27:41). Yeshua, being a "son of Jacob" knew this historical reality and addressed it by speaking to it, not ignoring or dismissing it. He equates this kind of speaking with faith (Emunah).

Yeshua spoke to the trees; some bore fruit while others dried up. He told His followers that if they wouldn't praise Him the "rocks would cry out." He lamented over Jerusalem asking why its inhabitants wouldn't receive Him. Yeshua seemed totally at ease speaking to the earth.

"But ask the wild animals, and they will teach you. Ask the birds of the heavens, and let them tell you. <u>Or speak to the earth</u>, and let it teach you. Let the fish of the sea make it known to you." Job 12:7-8

If you feel compelled to speak to the earth, you may feel foolish at first. Remember, the land is crying out more than YHWH's people.

Be sure to speak with kindness and respect. Never speak in an abusive manner, with arrogance, or in ignorance (of history or current situation). Do not pray amiss (see James 4:3). Prayer walking is not ego based.

Indigenous people (or people with direct authority) ought to be included and prayer walks. They have the authority to deal with ancient defilements that may exist on the land. We don't, however, have to think only of large areas of land for prayer walking. Your own property, church property, business property, and neighborhood present significant opportunities to speak to the earth.

Sometimes these prayer times will include singing, hand-clapping, drumming, dancing, or other physical activities as directed by Ruach HaKodesh. These actions and words may not always be understood by the participants, on-lookers, or other and their significance may not be understood until much later. The spirit-world (unseen good and bad spirits) understands and will respond to what is being spoken. The bad rulers and enthroned princes respond with fear to these acts of obedience. The scriptures speak of many times when weak and foolish things were used by YHWH to rout the enemy.

We cannot over emphasize that you begin with the healing of your personal land (yourself) and the cleansing of your own heart before you attempt to heal the land. Begin with your own life, family, and property before heading out to high places of the earth.

Dr. Jack Deere (conference 1998 in Fairbanks, AK) said, *"The prophetic is not what will happen but what ought to happen."* In other words, people must cooperate with YHWH's instructions if their speaking is to have integrity and effectiveness. Sometimes YHWH speaks a word that is immutable, something which cannot be hindered or prevented from occurring. Speaking to the earth requires faith, obedience, courage, and vision. It is worth it!

In a mission's conference in the mid-sixties, I head Dr. Don Hillis say, *"You only really believe that which activates you."* What a profound statement! Our active participation is required for YHWH's land to be healed. He has determined that healing the land will be an activity of partnership with

Him. We co-labor with Him on behalf of His earth. What a privilege and honor!

Note the active belief in these scriptures:

"Five of you will go after a hundred. A hundred of you will go after ten thousand. And those who hate you will fall in front of you by the sword." Leviticus 26:8

"Again I tell you this: if two of you agree on earth about anything you pray for, it will be done for you by My Father in heaven." Matthew 18:19

YHWH is looking for His stewards to speak to the earth and take action for the sake of His people and for the earth. We can do this without the need for titles (prophet etc.) and recognition but with humility, resolve, and faithful obedience.

I looked for a man among them who would build up the wall and stand before Me in the place where it is broken (in the gap), to stop Me from destroying the land, but I found no one." Ezekiel 22:30

We must understand that our Creator is a pro-active One (Echad). Hear Him:

"Obey the Word of YHWH. If you only hear and do not act, you are only fooling yourself." James 1:22

"For we work together with YHWH. You are YHWH's field."

1 Corinthians 3:9

"We are working together with YHWH. We ask you from our hearts not to receive YHWH's loving favor (grace) and then waste it." 2 Corinthians 6:1

"I make the word of My servant (steward) sure, and act upon the words of the men who speak for Me." Isaiah 44:26

Never underestimate the value of speaking to the earth!

What may appear foolish to us and others may be what is necessary for the healing of the land.

What is the ultimate value of speaking to the earth?

It is the deliverance and salvation of those who live on the land. After the prophet Ezekiel is told to speak to the earth, the hills, the valleys, the cities, etc. YHWH gives Ezekiel and Israel His promise:

"Adonai Elohim says, "I will also let the people of Israel ask Me to do this for them: I will give them many people, like the sheep of a flock."

Ezekiel 36:37

Healing the land is for the purpose of increasing the Kingdom of YHWH. Make it as difficult as possible for people to go to hell and as easy as possible for them to enter heaven.

Those who speak to the earth often find themselves becoming gatekeepers. The next chapter will help us understand what gatekeeping is and what gatekeepers do.

Chapter Four

Keeping the Gates

"The priests and the Levites made themselves holy (kadosh), and they made the people, the gates, and the wall holy." Nehemiah 12:30

"And he (King Solomon) chose who should be the gate-keepers at each gate." 2 Chronicles 8:14

"These leaders of the families who were set apart as gate-keepers were given duties like their brothers who work in Adonai's Temple."

1 Chronicles 26:12

Gatekeeping is simply establishing a physical or spiritual immigration policy. Every territory or area of ground has an entrance and exit place on it. Those places are the "gates" of that territory. Every gate is supposed to have a gatekeeper tending it.

Some gatekeepers are legitimate and possess invested and proper authority upon the land and over their gate. Others are pseudo and pretend gatekeepers who exert false authority over stolen or hijacked gates.

"The Ruach HaKodesh (Spirit) lifted me up and brought me to the east gate of Adonai's house which faces eastward. There I saw twenty-five men at the door of the gate. Then He said to me, "Son of man, these are the men who make sinful plans and tell others in this city to do what is wrong." Isaiah 11:1-2

What are true gatekeepers?

True gatekeepers are disciples of Yeshua and possess rightful authority to allow influences onto their property through opened gates, and to prevent evil influences out by closed gates. They have no need to announce their station or pronounce their authority; they do not become controllers or power seekers; they are not territorial but simply open and close doors/gates. They are servants serving with humility, compassion, integrity, vision, and resolve.

Inuit Elder — Oil by Sungiima

"On your walls, O Jerusalem, I have put men to keep watch (gatekeepers). All day and all night they will never be quiet." Isaiah 62:6

Everyone is a gatekeeper at some level; fathers/mothers, husbands/wives are gatekeepers of their households. Apostles, prophets, pastors, evangelists, and teachers are gatekeepers of their local fellowships or gatherings. Mayors and council members are gatekeepers of their communities. First Nations people, specifically their Chiefs, are gatekeepers of their nations and continents.

Not every gatekeeper is a disciple of Yeshua and sometimes they are gatekeepers over our lives. The scriptures instruct us to intercede for our government officials, as gatekeepers, they can allow both good and evil to enter the gates of our communities.

We are gatekeepers of our own hearts (minds). We have the authority of autonomy and can allow good, proper into our lives and keep unholy things out. This is accomplished by the function of our mind, will, and emotions.

Note how King David (Psalm 101) was gatekeeping his own life:

"I <u>will</u> sing (his gatekeeping uses the word "will") of lovingkindness and of what is right and fair. I <u>will</u> sing praises to You, O YHWH."

I <u>will</u> be careful to live a life without blame. When will You come to me? I <u>will</u> walk within my house with a right and good heart.

I <u>will</u> set no sinful thing in front of my eyes. I hate the work of those who are not faithful. It <u>will</u> not get hold of me.

A sinful heart <u>will</u> be far from me. I <u>will</u> have nothing to do with sin.

I <u>will</u> stop whoever talks against his neighbor in secret. I <u>will</u> not listen to anyone who has a proud look and a proud heart.

My eyes <u>will</u> look in favor on the faithful of the land, so they may serve me. He who walks without blame <u>will</u> help me.

He who ways are false <u>will</u> not live in my house. He who tells lies <u>will</u> not stand in front of me.

I will destroy all the sinful in the land every morning. I will cut off all those who do wrong from the city of Adonai."

That is a significant list of gatekeeping values to which the King is committed. He won't speak gossip nor listen to it. Whenever David uses the words "I will," he is making a gate-keeping decision. That is true gatekeeping.

Becoming a diligent and faithful personal gatekeeper precedes all other gatekeeping duties. There exist hundreds of scriptures addressing the domain of personal holiness and righteousness.

The scriptures speak of "the gate of heaven (cf. Genesis 28:17)," and the "gates of hell (cf. Matthew 16:18)." It also speaks of many earthly or city gates and identifies many of them.

Why were city gates so important?

The city gates were used as places for public debate, reading of the law, making proclamations, and holding court hearings. City leaders and elders met there to make decisions about their city. The priests and prophets would prophesy at the gate (cf. Isaiah 29:21; Amos 5:10; Jeremiah 17:1). The gates were the entrance of all trade and commerce for the city. They were diligently guarded every night against thieves, spies, and enemies.

In Jerusalem there were twelve city gates, each having a different function:

The sheep gate – Nehemiah 3:1 The Sheep Gate is the entrance where the lambs, which were used for the temple sacrifices, were brought into the city. Yeshua referred to Himself as the Sheep Gate (see John 10), as all who enter the Holy City must enter through Him.

Some congregations and fellowships function as Sheep Gates for their community. This gate is characterized by self-denial and people constantly make huge personal sacrifices for the sake of the Kingdom of Heaven. Sheep Gate congregations aren't normally large.

The valley gate – Nehemiah 2:13; 3:13 The Valley Gate overlooked the Hinnom Valley, also referred to as Gehenna, or the place of eternal torment. This valley was a place of defilement, idolatry, the sacrificial fires to Molech, and the collection area for the city's sewage. Not a pretty place.

This gate reminds us that we've passed from death to life through Yeshua HaMeshiach. We also need to pass from life to death. This is called the sanctification process. We get the "sewage" out of our lives and get "brain-washed."

Some congregations concentrate their efforts and teaching on this process, usually through counseling services. They help people strengthen their walk along the path of beauty. When people are "washed" clean, they find hope and value for their futures.

The well gate – Nehemiah 2:14; 3:15 This gate is also called the "Fountain Gate." It is near the Pool of Siloam where Yeshua sent the blind man to wash (cf. John 9:7). Water from this Pool was brought to the Temple in a golden vessel during the Feast of Tabernacles.

The pool was fed by a conduit which started at a spring near the Water Gate. Spring water is referred to as "living water" because its source is not a well or cistern.

This gate reminds us of the "washing of the water of the Torah (Word) (Ephesians 5:26)."

Well Gate congregations focus on teaching and have many schools offering programs for instruction. Probably many seminaries are the results of Well Gate congregations.

The water gate – Nehemiah 3:26 This gate is located near the only source of fresh water for the whole city of Jerusalem. Since the spring for this water source was outside the city wall, a conduit was cut through 1,780 feet of solid rock and the water emptied in to the Pool of Siloam. This fresh water was available to those within the city gates but not to the enemies outside the gate.

What a beautiful reminder of the fullness and outpouring of the Ruach HaKodesh. In this same context the scriptures says, "This is what Yeshua said about the Ruach HaKodesh (cf.John 7:37)."

Some congregations function as literal conduits for believers wanting to know and experience more of the Ruach HaKodesh in their lives.

The fish gate – Nehemiah 3:3 At this gate the fish for the local market were brought into the city. Likely because of the fishermen's desire to keep their catch as fresh as possible, they were assigned only one gate for their products. During King David's reign this gate was called "the Gate of Ephraim (2 Kings 14:13)." Ephraim means "double portion" and represents the blessing of YHWH upon believer's lives.

"Instead of your shame you will have a double portion (an Ephraim)." Isaiah 61:7-20)

May YHWH give us a "double portion" as we "fish" for mankind with our efforts of love, compassion, and respect for them.

The old gate – Nehemiah 3:6 Some scholars believe the Old Gate belonged to Salem which was first built by King Melchizedek (see Genesis 14).

Have you noticed how we serve a YHWH of history? He refers to Himself as "the Elohim of Abraham, Isaac, and Jacob." While we continue to become "new" and "renewed," we must remember the ancient paths and return to them (see Jeremiah 6:16). Yeshua said, *"The faithful scholar brings out his house treasures both old and new* (Matthew 13:52)."

Some congregations are great at preserving the faithful traditions of the scriptures and the Body of Messiah. They offer us a sense of the validity of history and seek to preserve the beauty of ceremonies that are precious from the past.

The dangers are obvious; these traditions can become icons considered equal with scripture itself leading to a kind of idolatry of its own making. They key is keeping the "old" things fresh and vibrant, full of Ruach HaKodesh and spiritual life.

The dung gate – Nehemiah 3:14 The dung gate was named because of the piles of rubbish in the Valley of Tophet below it. The garbage from the city was always burned outside the city.

This gate represents the renunciation of all flesh or carnality. Rabbi Shaul wrote, *"I consider everything a loss (rubbish, dung) compared to the surpassing greatness of knowing Meshiach Yeshua, my Adonai."*

Philippians 3:10

The sacrifices were also burned outside the city, just as Yeshua suffered "outside the city." (Hebrews 13:12)

This gate is not a popular one in the Body of Messiah. These congregations focus on helping people get the "dung" out of their lives. They have a lot of counseling, pot-luck food services, some homeless shelters, addiction services, etc. They are willing to serve many broken and dysfunctional people. Their service in the Body of Messiah is so necessary and wonderful.

The horse gate – Nehemiah 3:28 This gate represents military strength or spiritual warfare. The actual Horse Gate was at the end of the bridge leading to the Temple.

Our spiritual weapons are not carnal or fleshly, filled with revenge or hatred (see 2 Corinthians 10), but remain mighty through YHWH. The scripture says, *"Some men trust in horses and chariots but we will remember Adonai our Elohim ."* Psalm 20:7

The Horse Gate reminds us that a real, spiritual battle exists for the souls of mankind. These gatekeepers are warriors involved in the battle. They are frontiersmen, watchmen, and trustworthy soldiers of the cross of Yeshua the Messiah.

YHWH establishes congregations to emphasize the nature of spiritual warfare and provide tools for proper and righteous battle. They are excellent at training intercessors, hosting conferences, seminars, and equipping believers through the "boot camp" of warfare.

The east gate – Nehemiah 3:29 This gate is commonly known as the "gate called beautiful (Acts 3:2)." It is regarded as a primary gate leading to the Temple. It was decorated with brass and precious metals and was the largest of the city gates.

The crippled beggar was miraculously healed at this gate (see Acts 3).

Today this gate is completely closed and sealed, waiting for the return of the Messiah as King of Kings. In Ezekiel's prophecy, we're told that through the East Gate the shekinah (glory) of Adonai entered and filled the Temple. Soon Adonai and King will return through that Eastern Gate.

Some congregations focus on the truths of the end times. They have their charts and maps, timetables and systems all worked out. Their word is always "Time is short."

YHWH is also establishing "East Gate" congregations that are able to release the shekinah (glory) of YHWH into the earth through their worship and praise. They restore His glorious names and keep them lifted up in their lives and gatherings.

The master gate – Nehemiah 3:31 This gate represents watching and praying, it is the Gate of the Guard. We can hear Yeshua's plaintive inquiry, *"Could you not watch and pray with Me for even a hour?"* Mark 14:34

He is asking His disciples to be gatekeepers with Him during an important hour of His life. Yeshua challenges the Body of Messiah to be "found watching and praying (Luke 12:37)."

Master Gate congregations are praying ones. They organize prayer watches and vigils throughout their communities. They host all-night prayer sessions; some even have 24/7 prayer groups.

Every believer ought to keep this gate vital and important in their personal lives of faith.

Some larger communities will have representations of these gates in them. Some congregations are so large they will have all the gates represented within their own structure or program.

Some congregations do not "get along" with others simply because they have not understood what their gate is compared to the gate across the street. For instance, the Fish Gate congregation doesn't understand why the Horse Gate congregation doesn't get off their "high horses" and come over and help them "bring in the net." The Master Gate intercessors "know" the Dung Gate congregation would need less counseling if they would just "pray more." You get the idea?

YHWH has blessed His earth with huge varieties of callings and gifts, including gatekeeping duties. If we could honor, respect, and embrace each gate, we could begin to understand what makes other groups "tick" and we would catch a glimpse of the bigger picture YHWH has for us and our communities.

People who move from "church to church" aren't necessarily dissatisfied. They are seeking to know, as gatekeepers, at what gate YHWH would position them. They may need help and encouragement in finding that gate, so be gracious and helpful.

The gates we've mentioned have both personal and corporate implications invested in them. YHWH will show you for which gate He has prepared you and He can and does reposition His stewards. YHWH is also setting up gates on a national and international scope. Some gates have such significance they impact entire continents. Some gatekeepers have international responsibilities such as feeding the poor or providing medical services, etc.

The scriptures make many references to gates and gatekeeping activities. Even heaven has twelve gates with the names of the tribes of Israel inscribed upon them. Do you know what tribe is yours' and what gate you should enter?

There are some gates that belong to everyone:

Gates of thanks-giving *"Go into His gates with thanksgiving and into His holy places with praise. Give thanks to Him. Honor His name."* Psalm 100:4

Thanksgiving is the gate that releases freedom in our personal relationship with YHWH. Psalm 95:2 says. *"Let us come before His presence with thanksgiving, and make a joyful noise to Him."*

The Gate of Thanksgiving has a gatekeeper and it is you and me. We gate-keep our own hearts and we can create generous opportunities for personal expressions of gratitude. Try beginning your day by thinking of ten things you're thankful for and ten people you're thankful for and see if your day seems brighter and better.

Gates of praise – *"Fighting will not be heard again in your land. Nothing in you land will be destroyed. You will call your walls Salvation (Yeshua) and your gates praise."* Isaiah 60:18

As with the Gates of Thanksgiving, the Gates of Praise reside within your own heart. You can open that gate by an act of your will.

Musical worship leaders ought to open the Gates of Praise before attempting to lead their congregations in worship.

Gates of truth – *"Open the gates, that the nation that is right with YHWH may come in, the one that keeps (nourishes) truth."* Isaiah 26:2

Truth is the expression of reality. Reality is experienced to the same degree that the Gates of Truth are opened in your heart and mind. Remember, **you are not transformed by the removal of your mind**. Rabbi Shaul wrote in Philippians 2:5, *"Let this mind be in you which was in Yeshua the Meshiach."* In other words, Yeshua doesn't have a Western mind. We're the ones needing to convert and begin think like Him and have His world-view. This "renewed" mind will allow us to know and love the truth.

"The coming of the lawless one is according to the working of Satan, with all power and signs and wonders of falsehood, and with all deceit of unrighteousness in those perishing, because they did not receive the love of the truth, in order for them to be saved." 2 Thessalonians 2:9-10

The Gates of Truth open up to a highway of freedom. *"You shall know the truth and the truth (Yeshua) shall make you free."* John 8:32

Gates of righteousness - *"Open to me the gates of righteousness and goodness. I will go through them and give thanks to Adonai. This is the gate of Adonai. Those who are right with YHWH will pass through it."*

Psalm 118:19-20

King David refers to the Gate of Righteousness as "the gates of Adonai." This is a relational aspect of YHWH's dealings with mankind. Holiness is doing what is right between you and YHWH. Righteousness is doing what is right between you and your fellowman.

Doing what is right between people groups opens their hearts to the path of beauty and grace. Obviously the contrary is also true. Acting abusively, oppressively, and destructively will close hearts to any meaningful spiritual exchange. We must open the Gates of Righteousness within ourselves to be able to embrace differences between people groups.

Understanding Gates

It requires some understanding of gates to appreciate what and how gatekeepers function.

For instance, when one looks at a map of North America, one can clearly see the route of the earliest migrations of First Nations people. The Northern Gates are along the Bering Straits that include Point Hope (the Northern most crossing), Kotzebue, the Diamede Islands, Nome area, and St. Lawrence Island. Because of long-term ice cover, people and animals were able to cross from Siberia into "North America (Turtle Island). As these early tribes migrated, they brought with them their knowledge of the Creator as revealed in the general revelation of YHWH to all peoples. Some tribes held this knowledge, protected it, and carefully nourished it. Some were not as , deception. Soon shamanism and animism were flourishing throughout the continent.

Shamanism had its roots in the Altei Region of Siberia and it migrated, as a religious philosophy, around the circumpolar nations in 1180 years. This was long before any modern travel, communications, or even the travels of the "discoverers." This shamanism seems to counterfeit the true apostolic ascension gifting of Yeshua to His disciples. Shamanism and its varying offshoots have had negative consequences in the lives of thousands of people since its inception.

True, apostolic gate-keepers will be necessary to close the gates of generational wickedness and open the Gates of Righteousness for the continents involved. Instead of bondage, fear, oppression, slavery, and deceit, we could see freedom, openness, truthfulness, and hope released upon the land.

Beverly Klopp writes in her book, *Ask of Me,* the following encouragement and hopes for First Nations people:

"The weakest of the poor (First Nations), the poorest of the poor, and the most disillusioned and oppressed of the nations shall soon rise to defeat that which has defeated them from their earliest beginnings. Through deep repentance, they shall have power in the Spirit to intercede, to preach, and to bring down evil forces that control the darkest areas on the earth – the Far East including U.S.A. I pray that one day the northwest shall send these precious Indian Nations to free and break the power of this shamanistic spirit and false godhead established over the people of the 10/40 window (10 degrees and 40 degrees latitude which includes the U.S.A.).

Beverly Klopp is correct is in stating that we "shall soon rise." This is indeed happening all over the world, wherever indigenous people live and in spite of the horrific historical scars they bear. First Nations people are "in-the-know" about spiritual things and what is required of them. Much of their deepest wisdom has lain bed-ridden in the dormitory of their souls, but an alarm bell from mother-nature has awakened the sleeping giant and this earth will not be the same.

George Otis Jr., the Director of the Sentinel Group, is a leader in this understanding of spiritual mapping which includes gatekeeping writes:

"The Sentinel Group announces a new initiative called the *Ancient Paths Project.* It is a cooperative effort in which Native and immigrant peoples will revisit altars and covenants. The research phase will involve discerning *ancient gateways* (geographic points of entry) that brought aboriginal people into various continents and nations; *ancient homelands* (early settlements) where nomadic clans incubated new languages, cultures, and spiritual pacts; *ancient pathways* (secondary migration routed) littered with ceremonial altars and high places; and *ancient stairways* (sacred sites that served as portals) a'la Jacob's ladder.

Throughout the year 2000, indigenous peoples will travel to sacred valleys, caves, rivers, petroglyphs, and mountains to roll up the red carpet their ancestors offered to demonic powers. After giving the old carpet a good dust off, they will replace it – this time as a warm welcome to the King of Glory." (The Sentinel Group Newsletter, Nov. 25, 1998)

What is gatekeeping really?

In the Hebrew language it is translated "thinking." A gatekeeper is one who makes decision based upon solid information gained from reliable research and discovery. Such thinking leads to exercising authority to open and close gates for the land and its people. Never be afraid to think!

When spiritual work is commenced, it is often easy to place emotion, expressional preferences, and spiritual clichés ahead of the hard work of thinking with a renewed mind. We can do hard things!

Sometimes people act before research is begun and that results in a stabbing-in-the-dark kind of effort. Do not seek answers for questions not yet posed. It is better to do things correctly than to assume we will have an opportunity to repeat it.

Many times a common phrase, actually a cliché, is used when prayer walking and speaking to the earth and that phrase is "taking authority," or "taking authority in the name of Yeshua." A person either has authority or doesn't have it. It can be given to others, shared with others, or represented with proper permission, but "taking" is stealing. Only gatekeepers can open gates of authority for others.

Have you noticed that those possessing authority seldom need to tell others, they simply function in their responsibility in a natural (super?) way. Those who don't really possess authority seem to try and convince others they have it. It can appear quite silly and superficial when people do this.

Authority is linked to protocol, treating one another with respect and honor. When respect and honor are guarded and recognized, freedom can be extended in many partnerships and endeavors.

The Purpose of Protocol

When a First Nations person traveled into other tribal territories, certain kinds of protocol were practiced. The reason for this being that the traveler did not possess authority upon the land in the same manner or to the same degree as those living on the land. The traveler would seek permission to travel, camp, hunt, or trade within the territory. This permission was sought from the highest authority in the land, the Chief, who was the gatekeeper of his nation.

An audience with the Chief would be sought, the mission stated, the length of stay, gifts and honors exchanged, and permission granted or withheld by the gatekeeper. With permission, the immigrant possessed a new measure of authority, not "taken" but "granted," to proceed to the desired destination or mission.

Yeshua practiced protocol and passed it on to His disciples in John 10:

"Truly, truly, I say to you, he who does not enter through the door (gate) into the sheepfold, but climbs up by another way, that one is a thief and a robber.

But he who enters through the door is the shepherd of the sheep.

The doorkeeper (gatekeeper) opens for him, and the sheep hear his voice. And he calls his own sheep by name and leads them out."

Here Yeshua calls those who refuse to enter through the gate and gatekeeper "thieves and robbers." Why? What have they stolen? They have stolen the authority of the gatekeeper assuming gates have no purpose or value.

Think is terms of modern missions' movements and ask, "How many mission agencies understood and used proper protocol to build bridges to the nations they were trying to reach?" Most simply "took authority" and forced the gospel message upon people who knew far more about YHWH than the missionaries imagined.

Protocol is a basic principle of humility. It is giving honor where honor is due.

Remember the time when Yeshua was welcomed into Jerusalem with shouts of "Hosanna, Hosanna!" and what happened next? With the protocol of welcome, He immediately proceded to the Temple where He cleansed the land and confronted the religious spirit, driving it from the Temple area.

Following protocol releases huge amounts of spiritual authority to get a mission completed and completed right.

As we speak or accomplish spiritual activities, the unseen rulers are paying close attention:

"So that now, through the assembly, the many-sided wisdom of Elohim might be known to the principalities and authorities in the heavenlies." Ephesians 3:10

According to Yeshua, if I refuse to go through gates and gatekeepers, that is, to honor with proper and acceptable protocol – I am a thief and robber. And as a thief, I become open to the severest attacks of the leaders and powers in heavenly places.

If I come through the gatekeeper, with acceptable protocol, evil spirits are prevented from unwarranted attacks on me or my mission.

What might have happened if missionaries had humbled themselves, followed protocol, gone through gatekeepers, and had been free from attacks of the enemy? What would their reports look and sound like?

I recall the profound experience I had when I submitted myself and ministry to the Grand-Chief of the largest nation in Alaska, the Athabascans. He opened his heart and territory to me and I immediately felt a release in my heart to accomplish my assignment. It was so freeing, and I knew the demonic spirits also knew that I had authority to do my spiritual mission among those villages.

Gates and gatekeeping are real issues. They can affect the entire nature of our spiritual efforts throughout the earth.

But what if the Chief has turned me away?

Ask yourself, "Who is the steward of the land – me or the Chief?"

"Who is the gatekeeper?"

More importantly, can I trust YHWH to make a way where there seems to be no way?

If our primary message is for people to "trust YHWH," then we must also trust Him. If we are unwilling to embrace gates and gatekeepers in our efforts for the Kingdom of Heaven, we do not trust YHWH, and we are nothing more than thieves and robbers consumed with our own ideas and sense of importance.

Rabbi Shaul writes, *"For a great and effective door has been opened to me, and many are opposing." 1 Corinthians 16:9*

Opened gates doesn't infer there will not be opposition, but the effect of that opposition can be diminished by the humility of understanding, embracing, and submitting to the gatekeepers YHWH has placed in the earth.

8 Commands to Gatekeepers

Isaiah 62:6-11

"I have set watchmen on your walls, O Jerusalem, all the day and all the night, continually, who are not silent. You who remember YHWH, give yourself no rest."

Do not be silent.

"and give Him no rest till He established and till He makes Jerusalem a praise in the earth."

Give YHWH no rest.

"Pass through, pass through the gates!"

Go through the gates.

"Prepare the way for the people."

Open a way for the people.

"Build up, build up the highway!"

Build up the road.

"Remove the stones."

Remove obstacles.

"Lift up a banner."

Raise a flag of victory.

"Say to the daughter of Zion, 'See, your deliverance has come."

Speak to the earth and its people.

This passage has many insights on gatekeeping. It encourages speaking, intercession, inclusion of gatekeepers in the blessings, serving, making a highway for YHWH, removing barriers, raising a flag of hope, and telling the good news – Yeshua is coming!

YHWH wants to appoint you as a gatekeeper in the area where you live, work and worship. Prepare your heart and mind for this important and strategic mission. Share with other gatekeepers and notice what YHWH is doing through them. Pray, fast, and prayer-walk your territory and speak to the earth as YHWH instructs. Become wise and filled with Divine understanding. YHWH will help you!

Humility, repentance, speaking to the earth, and gatekeeping indicates the need for understanding spiritual mapping. The following chapter presents a brief overview of this enthralling work in the Kingdom.

Chapter Five

Spiritual Mapping

Spiritual mapping is the phrase used to describe the demographic, geographic, historical, and spiritual inventory of the root bondages manifesting themselves through prevailing bondages in the land and people where you and I live.

The purpose of spiritual mapping is simply this: informed intercession.

For too long the Body of Messiah has prayed what it "felt" like praying without a strategic plan based on real histories and pertinent facts. There has been no follow-up nor any assessment as to the effectiveness of the prayers.

From the last chapter we can see that gatekeeping has been happening for decades of our continent. Many of these gatekeepers were not careful to keep evil out of their lands and ancient defilements were allowed to flourish on the land.

Where records of such defilements can be obtained, they should be noted for prayer walks and other spiritual activities. Local "church" histories should be examined and the land where spiritual buildings stand should be made free of all defilements.

Spiritual histories are not all negative. YHWH has accomplished many significant things amongst varieties of people groups. Where blessing has occurred, people need to be interviewed and records kept, not for the sake of record keeping, but, again, for informed intercession. The positive aspects of YHWH's blessing can significantly affect the praise and worship in the Body of Messiah.

"Send men to spy (spiritual mapping) out the land of Canaan, which I am giving to the children of Israel. Send one man from each tribe of their fathers, everyone a leader among them.

Waiting *oil by Sungiina*

And Moses sent them to spy out the land of Canaan, and said to them, "Go up here into the land of the South, and go up to the mountains, and see what the land is like, and the people who dwell in it, whether strong or weak, whether few or many, and whether the land they dwell in is good or evil, whether the cities they inhabit are in camps or strongholds, and whether the land is rich or poor, and whether there are forests there or not. And you shall be strong, and bring some of the fruit of the land." Numbers 13:2, 17-20

Did YHWH ask them to spiritually map the "promised land" because He didn't know what was there? Of course not. He asked them so they would obtain a vision, with evidence, of His intentions to bless and help them occupy this new (old) land. His desire was to help them see what they would possess but they had to map it first.

The mapping YHWH asked of Israel was to prepare the entire nation, not just the spies or the leaders of Israel. Spiritual mapping is not for the mappers only but for the entire Body of Messiah.

"A wise one scales the city of the mighty, and brings down trusted strongholds." Proverbs 21:22

"The words of the wise, spoken calmly, should be heard rather than the shout of a ruler of fools. Wisdom is better than weapons of conflict, but one sinner destroys much good." Ecclesiastes 9:17-18

Spiritual warfare, similar to military conquest, requires diligent and informed strategic planning, using reliable information. It's not merely how one feels about a place but why one feels that way. Is there evidence to confirm one's feelings, and does the evidence suggest a wise plan to change the environment. If not, can one adjust their feelings to match the evidence?

Yeshua did some rather interesting spiritual mapping with the seven churches of Asia Minor (see Book of Revelation chapters 2 -3). He noted their strengths and complimented them for them, but He also noted their weaknesses and blessed them with warnings so they could avert the hidden dangers they couldn't see. Not once did Yeshua curse them, but lovingly appealed to them so they could benefit from His knowledge about them.

George Otis Jr. defines spiritual mapping as a process designed;

"...to help Christian workers see the mission field as it really is – not as it appears to be. The process involves monitoring and assessing the implications of current trends and development related to: the times in which we live; the spiritual battlefield on which we fight; God's working in evangelism and spiritual warfare – but it is not magic. It is subjective in that it is a skill that is born out of right relationship with God and a love for His world. It is objective in that it can be verified (or discredited by history, sociological observation and God's Word). Ibid., The Sentinel Group

Spiritual mappers are dedicated stewards seeking freedoms for others who may or may not appreciate their efforts or believe what they discover. Some of the most hurtful hits mappers take are from other believers who simply refuse to face the facts presented to them.

Every mapper must begin by believing that YHWH has a sovereign plan for his or her community, nation, and continent. They must also believe He has the right and authority to share or withhold His plan according to His own purposes. It is our privilege to inquire of Him but we must submit to His will for our community.

It's about reaching lost people. It's about praying effectively with informed intercession. Beyond that it becomes busy work.

Sometimes we are mapping and don't even realize it. Of course, before the term was coined, many people were mapping their areas.

From Daniel Kikawa's e-mail to me about an Amazon trip:

"Eruera is a tribal leader of the Maori (New Zealand Indigenous People). Axa is a religious leader of the Suruwaha tribe. Eruera grew up on a sunny island of the Pacific. Axa grew up in the Amazon rain forest. Both are strong, brown-skinned and used to the challenges of the forest. They are also both very much concerned about spiritual things.

Eruera is a world-traveler who has visited many different peoples and cultures. Axa has never left the region of the Coxodoa River. He hasn't even visited the nearest Brazilian settlement.

Eruera's people have heard the gospel for many years. Axa's tribe lives oppressed by spirits of suicide, and believing that the whole tribe will kill themselves in a group-suicide ritual.

Among the Suruwaha, Axa was the first to have an encounter with Jesus. Jesus appeared to him on a jungle trail when Axa was running to get some poison root in order to kill himself. He saw Jesus wearing a loin cloth and with His body covered with paint. Jesus spoke softly in perfect Suruwaha telling Axa not to kill himself. Axa belived Jesus, abandoned his suicidal compulsion and has grown spiritually. But the Suruwaha people continued to serve the "Kunaha karuji" or the "Spirit of Poison."

They say that long ago a witch doctor invoked the spirit of death. Since then this spirit who wants this tribe to serve him has oppressed them. They don't know anyone who knows how to drive out the spirit of death.

When the Maori heard of the struggle of the Suruwaha, they decided to cross the ocean in a long trip to perform an occidental ceremony of their people. They decided to offer spiritual help to the Suruwaha tribe through the "Haka" (prophetic dance) ceremony, a tribal ritual that has as its purpose rebuking death.

It is a powerful religious ceremony during which they sing and dance, call on the name of Jesus, and rebuke the spirit of death. Today this ritual has been used by the Maori as a powerful weapon of spiritual warfare. The Maori want to expulse the "Kunaha karuji" and prophesy life to the Suruwaha.

A picture of a Taiaha (Maori fighting stick) was shown to the Suruwaha. They told the missionaries, who showed them that picture, they have a prophecy in their tribe that says the people who would bring this stick would break the spirit of death over the tribe. Thus, the Maori are going to the Suruwaha to fulfill a prophecy that will set the people free through the death and resurrection of Christ who has defeated death!"

This happened in the spring of 1999. One could make a great list of spiritual mapping ideas from just this one account.

There is both ancient and contemporary history at work. There are ancient curses and contemporary defilements. God shows up on the scene and intervenes on behalf of the tribe. The Maori respond, etc. It's great!

(Note: a later report speaks of complete success of the journey by the Maori with many of Suruwaha becoming believers and the spirit of death defeated.)

Here is a report from Charles Colson's *Breakpoint Commentary* – April 26, 1999:

"It was a test all of us would hope to pass, but none of us really wants to take. A masked gunman points his weapon at a Christian and asks, "Do you believe in God?" She knows that if she says "yes" she'll pay with her life. But unfaithfulness to her Lord is unthinkable. So, with what would be her last words, she calmly answers, "Yes, I believe in God."

What makes this story remarkable is that the gunman was no communist thug, nor was the martyr a Chinese pastor. As you may have guessed, the event I'm describing took place last Tuesday in Littleton, Colorado.

As the Washington Post reported, the two students who shot 13 people, Eric Harris and Dylan Klebold, did not choose their victims at random – they were acting out of a kaleidoscope of ugly prejudices.

Media coverage has centered on the killer's hostility toward racial minorities and athletes, but there was another group the pair hated every bit as much, if not more: Christians. And there were plenty of them to hate at Columbine High School.

According to some accounts, eight Christians were killed. Among them was Cassie Bernall. And it was Cassie who made the dramatic decision I've just described – fitting for a person whose favorite movie was "Braveheart," in which the hero dies a martyr's death.

Cassie was a 17-year-old junior with long blond hair, hair she wanted to cut off and have made into wigs for cancer patients who had lost their hair through chemotherapy. She was active at Westpool's Community Church and was known for carrying her Bible to school. Cassie was in the school library reading her Bible when the two young killers burst in.

Cassie's martyrdom was even more remarkable when you consider that just a few years ago she had dabbled in the occult, including witchcraft. She had embraced the same darkness and nihilism that drove her killers to such despicable acts. But two years ago, Cassie dedicated her life to Christ, and turned her life around. Her friend, Craig Moon, called her a "Light for Christ." Well, this "light for Christ" became a rare American martyr of the 20th century. Cassie's brother Chris found a poem Cassie had written just two days prior to her death. It read:

Now I have given up on everything else

I have found it to be the only way

To really know Christ and to experience

The mighty power that brought

Him back to life again, and to find

Out what it means to suffer and to

Die with Him. So, whatever it takes

I will be the one who lives in the fresh

Newness of life of those who are

Alive from the dead.

What a positive and inspiring account of faith. But spiritual mapping includes both the positive and negative aspects of spiritual realities. Life isn't one-sided. If we are to accomplish significant things for YHWH, we must look at life from both sides and see what's really there.

In this account, if we had left the spiritual mapping to the media alone, we would have missed the hatred of the killers toward Christians. We would have missed the powerful testimony Cassie gave of her faith in the Messiah.

We would have missed many things important to understanding the incident, the condition of Columbine High School, and the future of Littleton, Colorado. With informed intercession, this community stands poised on the edge of a huge revival by Ruach HaKodesh.

Victor Lorenzo, in his materials, *"Evangelizing a City Dedicated to Darkness,"* gives these principles for spiritual mapping:

1. We must base our ministry on God's work and His revelation.
2. We must be certain we are living in holiness before we go forth.
3. We must be sent by God in His time and with His authority.
4. We must conduct our research according to the instructions we've received.
5. We must report our information without personal or prejudicial opinions.
6. We must keep an attitude of faith in the power of God.

Read the e-mail account from Michelle in Canada:

"I sat at my computer reading the e-mail report from Suuqiina about the "Gold Rush" in Alaska (about gold teeth fillings). Well, I sat reading and when I came to the part calling forth gold, I just agreed in prayer. After, I went to bed and never thought anything more about it.

The next morning as I was going about my usual routine, I heard this still-small voice saying, "Go check your teeth." I'm thinking, "Hmmmmmm." This went on 4-5 times during the day. Finally at about 4 p.m., I gave in and went to check. Sure enough, a gold film type layer was over three of my bottom teeth. I went to the kitchen and asked my 9-year-old son, Jesse, what color my fillings were. He told me, "Gold!" He asked me how I got them and asked if his were gold.

A young friend from Wales came over briefly and asked, "Where did you get those?" Well, I told him the story and he read the e-mail, which he wanted to send to his parents overseas. All over the world the Spirit is moving.

I also noticed that something very great has changed within me. I can't pin-point it, but I feel it may be pertaining to the gospel of peace. I feel that my mouth has been slowed down, if that makes sense. A great peace has come over me not to speak as I used to, Yet there's a caution for words and a very deep, unexplainable, passion for the Lord and for a quietness within that I had to come to, to be given the deep intercession for the First Nations people. I truly feel the Lord has quieted my soul. He is so good!"

One can trace the hand of YHWH's blessing upon His people and making every effort to help them see Him in the beauty of His shekinah (glory). He also brought about an attitude change and adjusted Michelle's spirit by imparting His shalom (peace) to her, which is worth much more than gold.

Learn to map the good and the bad. Look for things that matter to YHWH but which also produce changes, verifiable changes in the community being mapped.

After the Church of Anchorage (Alaska) was formed, we can document the change in crime statistics (downward), healings (upward), deliverances (upward), and salvations (upward).

A major breakthrough has occurred at the Ketchikan Correctional Institute (now fondly referred to as the Ketchikan Christian Institute) with many inmates serving Adonai as intercessors. The unity amongst the churches there is like never before.

These are not insignificant changes as Alaska, as a gatekeeping State to the continent, must have certain kinds of spiritual prototypes occurring within her.

Just as a river must flow from its source at the headwaters, the spiritual must flow from its source. The spiritual mapping of Alaska is now being accomplished for future targeting in intercession.

"Wisdom gives more strength to a wise man than ten rulers have in a city." *Ecclesiastes 7:19*

"Why does darkness linger where it does?" So asks George Otis Jr. in his book *The Twilight Labyrinth*.

I suppose we could ask the contrary: "Why does the light hang around in places unwanted?"

It requires more than information to answer such questions. It takes wisdom that comes from above. It will require anointing by Ruach HaKodesh to discover what the information is telling us.

Think as much as you can; research as carefully and diligently as possible, plot, graph, read, pray, get excited, get angry, get going – but leave plenty of room for Ruach HaKodesh to speak His mind on these things and "lead us into all the truth." He really does have something to say about spiritual mapping.

Don't consider doing spiritual mapping without trained and seasoned intercessors to help you. This is a partnership with many gifts and callings required to be involved. Keep your pastors and overseers informed on what you are researching and why. Give them plenty of room to decide what to do with your hard-earned information. Maybe they can use it, maybe they can't, or maybe they won't. Do your mapping in obedience and not merely for results or for the appreciation of others.

Remember, spiritual mapping is not about being clever or cute with information. It's about informed intercession. It is NOT spiritual warfare; rather, it helps everyone involved in the battle and those manning their spiritual gates. Stay as humble in mapping as you were in repentance. YHWH is Victor!

"The Holy Spirit was given to us as a promise that we will receive everything God has for us. God's Spirit will be with us until God finishes His work of making us complete. God does this to show His shining greatness." *Ephesians 1:14, New Life Version*

In the following chapter we will discover YHWH's provision for the anointing (His personal presence) of Ruach HaKodesh. Without His presence we are "dead-in-our-tracks." He has been so faithful to bring us to these truths and He will continue! Rejoice and have faith

Reindeer

Chapter Six

The Presence of YHWH

Here is one definition of the term "anointing:"

The unmistakable evidence, accompanied by appropriate manifestations, that YHWH's presence abides in one's life and upon one's mission.

"Elohim also bearing witness both with signs and wonders, with various miracles, and gifts of the Ruach HaKodesh, distributed according to His own desire." Hebrews 2:4

We don't believe YHWH has erected any barriers to His anointing. If barriers exist they are barriers we have erected. We are the ones that hinder or diminish YHWH's presence upon our lives.

We don't believe there exists a limited quantity of His presence and once it's consumed people desiring Him are somehow excluded. His presence is available to every follower of His. There remains no shortage of anointing.

We're only going to mention three possible barriers to His presence in this chapter. There are multitudes of them and many authors have written extensively on the subject.

These three barriers have a significant impact on healing the land. They appear to be the ones that are universal to all believers and have to be confronted and eliminated before proceeding on to the greater work YHWH has in mind for His stewards.

Here I must give credit to Rev. Sundar Krishnan for his insights on these first two passages of scripture. I heard him present these truths at a conference many years ago and have never forgotten them.

Stop working for YHWH without listening to YHWH.

Read it again and again until it firmly takes root in your thinking. The scripture passage is from Isaiah 55:

"Oh everyone who thirsts, come to the waters. And you who have no silver, come, buy and eat. Come, buy wine and milk without silver and without price.

Why do you weigh out silver for what is not bread, and your labor for what does not satisfy? Listen, listen to Me, and eat what is good, and let your being delight itself in fatness." (verses 1-2)

YHWH presents us with a new and strange economy. No money, no price tags, but we are challenged to "buy." Imagine going to your local grocery store and there are no price tags on the wine, milk, or bread and when you approach to pay they won't accept and money. How would you "buy" your merchandise?

The currency is **listening** – the rate of exchange is **time**. What wonderful concepts, but can we really afford both listening and time?

The Hebrew word for "listen" is *shema (the same as used in the Shema recited by Hebrew believers everywhere – "Hear (Shema) Oh Israel, YHWH your YHWH is one (Echad)."*

It means several important things; to hear with intelligence; to hear and apply in obedience; to hear with diligence and undivided attention. YHWH is serious about His economy because it is the economy of His Kingdom.

Without taking the time to listen to YHWH, we raise a huge barrier to His presence (anointing).

We may think that healing the land is primarily about sin, speaking to the earth, spiritual mapping, etc. but it's really more about our relationship with the Creator of the land and of us. It's not about ministry or mission first – it's about Him!

Please remove the idea that YHWH is preparing you for mission or ministry first. **He is preparing you for an eternity with Him first!** That will require both listening and time.

We have time to do what we want – right? Think about it. If we really want to do something we will sacrifice whatever is necessary and make time for it. Therefore, we can certainly make time for YHWH. It is worth it.

Again, **His currency is listening – the rate of exchange is time.**

"Incline your ear, and come to Me. Hear, so that your being lives. And let Me make an everlasting covenant with you, the trustworthy kindnesses of David." (verse 3)

In these first three verses, four times we've been challenged to listen. These words don't have the same meanings, however similar they might appear.

The word "listen" in verse 2 is the simple act of hearing sound. It is the frequencies of the words being spoken as they impact our ear drums and are translated into sounds that make sense to us. It is an important beginning.

The word "listen" in verse 3 means something special. In some translations it is written: "Incline your ear." I can only interpret it with a story from own family life.

When our daughter was in high school, she held a job, has a boyfriend, and had a social along with being an honor student. Her life was busy, busy, and more busy. We didn't see much of one another although we lived in the same house.

Every once in a while she would come into my office, plop down on my lap, throw her arms around my neck and give me a big kiss on the cheek. Guess what I would ask her? You're absolutely correct. "Honey, what do you want?" You're correct again – money for some project or some serious need.

I don't believe I ever turned her down, although I couldn't always give the desired amount. I wanted to model the generous giving Spirit of our Abba (father). This little account demonstrates this word "incline your ear" in the Hebrew language.

YHWH wants us to jump into His lap, throw our arms around His neck, give Him a big kiss and He'll ask us, "What do you want?" You'd better be ready with your answer because with YHWH Yireh that's a serious question and He is not poor.

If you've entered His Kingdom economy by listening and spending intimate time with Him, there's hardly anything He won't do for you (see John 15:7). He loves you, He likes you, and He is not poor! Listen, incline your ear to Him.

The last word "hear" is an action word. It's being ready for YHWH to speak and doing whatever He says – intentionally, diligently and immediately. This word YHWH roots in His historical covenant with King David and promises to make the same covenant with us. He is a covenant keeping YHWH!

How can we not afford these promises and provisions when the investment costs so little – listening to Him and spending time with Him?

"See, I have given Him as a witness to the people, a Leader and a Ruler for the people." (verse 4)

Here are three anointing's connected to this listening process; a witness; a commander; and a ruler.

A witness is a person who tells the truth about what he has seen or heard. No more, no less. YHWH has called everyone to be a witness of Him and for Him (see Acts 1:8). We don't have to make things up, we just have to tell truth about what we've seen and heard in our before and after our encounters with YHWH.

Then He calls some to be commanders (leaders). A leader is a person who tells the truth about what he has seen or heard in such a way that others follow him/her.

Rabbi Shaul was a leader: *"And what you have learned and received and heard and saw in me, practice these, and the Elohim of peace shall be with you."* *Philippians 4:9*

It takes an anointing (YHWH's presence) to be able to legitimately draw people to yourself and for them to want to follow you. These kinds of leaders are not made in leadership seminars alone. They are mostly prepared through the humility of listening and spending time with the real Leader of all – YHWH.

The third anointing is called a "Ruler." A ruler is a person who tells the truth in such a way that others follow him/her, and they tell it with divinely supported authority.

YHWH doesn't promote too many rulers as He's not having many "Chiefs and not many Indians." Rulership is a special anointing but the criteria remains the same, listening to YHWH and spending time with Him.

"See, a nation you do not know you shall call, and a nation who does not know you run to you, because of YHWH, your Elohim, and the Holy One of Israel, for He has adorned you." (verse 5)

YHWH rewards listening and time by opening doors of opportunity which in the natural, with our own methods, we could never open. He has always been a YHWH Who makes a way where there is no way.

Beyond all that He endows with His splendor allowing us to appear better than we are. What grace and mercy He shows us!

"Seek YHWH while He is to be found, call on Him while He is near." (verse 6)

YHWH invites us to the anointing of proximity. He would love it if we were to find Him and call upon Him in His nearness. He longs to be near to His faithful stewards.

Note how YHWH expands our opportunities; He began with listening to Him and spending time with Him, and now He adds "seeking" and "calling." He is abundant and willing to "give beyond what we think or imagine."

So now we're listening, spending time, seeking, and calling – Wow! We are so blessed by our Creator's love!

Finding YHWH and understanding His nearness implies Divine appointments with Him. He is increasing His Divine appointments in these last days for those who are open with their time and schedules. If we become rigid, agenda bound, and selfish with our personal availability, we cannot flow with the Ruach HaKodesh. His appointments become rare. However, if we are flexible, willing to flow with Him, and in tune with the harmony of His schedule, and hearing His voice, He creates Divine appointments for us. That's a pretty good deal!

"Let the wrong forsake his way, and the unrighteous man his thoughts. Let him return to YHWH, Who has compassion on him, and to our Elohim, for He pardons much." (verse 7)

He is not referring to the kinds of sins that defile the land. The wrong-doing here is working for YHWH without listening to YHWH. To work for Him without listening is trying to accomplish our mission without His direct involvement. That can be tragic and unnecessary. Note that this is not merely about what we are doing, but includes how we are thinking. We need renewed minds for this.

YHWH's promise is a full pardon and His compassion. He understands our desire to serve Him, but He wants us to serve Him His way and not ours. Again, it's about listening and spending time – it's about His Kingdom economy.

"For My thoughts are not your thoughts, neither are My ways your ways, declares YHWH. For as the heavens are higher than the earth, so are My ways higher than your ways, and My thoughts than your thoughts." (verses 8 and 9)

Here is Divine contrast and comparison. Our ways and thoughts don't measure up, but nevertheless, for whatever reasons, we insist on having our own way. What a huge barrier we raise to His presence when we do that. How it must grieve Him to see us make our puny attempts when He is ready to forgive, endow with splendor, open doors to nations, make covenants, and establish Divine appointments for us if we would but simply turn from our own ways and thoughts.

"For as the rain comes down (yarah-to cast down), and the snow from the heavens, and do not return there, but water the earth, and make it bring forth and bud, and give seed to the sower and bread to the eater." (verse 10)

YHWH shows us that the elements of the weather obey His purpose and He tells of the abundance of harvest they produce by merely listening for His command to rain or snow on the earth.

We recall YHWH's question of verse 2, "Why do we spend money for what is not bread?" The rain and snow produce seed and bread simply by falling upon the earth.

In the Hebrew language the term "torah" comes from a root word which means to "cast down." So this rain and snow example sets up the following verse about His Word. A father "casts down" (points) his arm to give instruction to his children. That's why the word "torah" is not "law" but rather "a father's instructions."

"So is My Word that goes forth from My mouth – it does not return to Me empty, but shall do what I please, and shall certainly accomplish what I sent it for." (verse 11)

His stated purpose is to have witnesses, leaders and rulers; all who have the same anointing of listening and spending time with YHWH. His Word is that I will have these kinds of stewards in the earth; My Word will not fail or be diminished in any manner. We can decide to be part of this important stewardship and fulfillment of His living Word (Torah).

"For with joy you go out, and with peace you are brought in – the mountains and the hills break forth into singing before you, and all the trees of the field clap the hands." (verse 12)

What a splendid return on our listening investment. Even the land itself joins in the celebration of obedience. This is healing the land! And it doesn't end with this.

"Instead of the thorn the cypress comes up, and instead of the nettle the myrtle comes up. And it shall be to YHWH for a name, for an everlasting sign which is not cut off." (verse 13)

Curse and barrenness are converted into abundance and fruitfulness. When your heart and mind becomes committed to YHWH's ways and thoughts (a renewed mind), He gives a harvest of a healed land as a sign of remembrance with lasting effects.

The cypress is a type of evergreen tree (no shedding of leaves or diminished service) which was used to craft musical instruments of worship. The nettle represents the "kings of the earth." The kings are not "listeners" except to their own musings. They are enemies of all that is of YHWH and His Torah.

The myrtle is a fruit (nut) tree that provides nourishment, shade, and abundant harvest. No wonder Yeshua is so often referred to as "the Branch."

We can remove the barrier of working for YHWH without listening to Him. How? By committing to becoming listeners.

2. **Stop working for YHWH without waiting upon YHWH.**

The text is Isaiah 64:1-7

"Oh, that You would tear the heavens open, come down, that mountains shall shake before You? – as when fire burns twigs, as fire makes water boil – to make Your Name known to Your adversaries, so that nations tremble before You." (verses 1-2)

This sounds very spiritual, but who should be shaking before Adonai? The Mountains? Who should be witnesses to the nations? YHWH? Here is a plaintive cry for YHWH to do what He has endowed His stewards to do.

"When You did awesome matters, which we did not expect, You came down, mountains did shake before You!" (verse 3)

Here is a wonderful description of revival – YHWH doing powerful things "we don't expect." One problem with modern day revivals is that we have them and YHWH all figured out. Our insistence upon repeating some historical revival eliminates YHWH's opportunity to do the unexpected. It would delight Him to be allowed to surprise us once in a while.

"Since the beginning of the ages they have not heard nor perceived by the ear, nor has eye seen any Elohim besides You, who acts for those who wait for Him." (verse 4)

When have our ears heard or our eyes seen the notion that YHWH would do the work if we would do the waiting?

Thus word "wait" is an <u>action</u> word not a passive one.

The Hebrew word "wait" here is "chahkah" and means to "adhere," "a hook,"and "to entwine by twisting (see Strong's #2442)."

To "wait" on YHWH means to get "hooked into Him," to "adhere" to Him, and to "entwine" ourselves with Him and not attempt to accomplish exploits apart from Him.

These are functions YHWH's stewards can do to insure His presence (anointing) upon their lives. Let's wait on Him!

"You shall meet him who rejoices and does righteousness, who remembers You in Your ways. See, You were wroth when we sinned in them a long time. And should we be saved?

And all of us have become as one unclean, and all our righteousnesses are as soiled rags. And all of us fade like a leaf, and our crookedness, like the wind, have taken us away." (verses 5 &6).

We don't believe the sins mentioned here are typical of defilements but rather specific in referring to working for YHWH without waiting upon Him.

Both right and good works are mentioned as being like "soiled rags," but they remain right and good ways in the perceptions of those doing them.

There appears to be many things that believers snatch from YHWH's Hand into their own without submitting to His timing or purpose.

When He asks "if we can be saved?,' He is speaking of rescuing us from our own efforts. Some we must lie in because they are what we have made. Because He is gracious and slow to anger, He rescues us more often than we realize. He is so good to us!

"And there is no one who calls on Your Name, who stirs himself up to take hold of You; for You have hidden Your face from us, and have consumed us because of our crookedness."

Here are three significant results of working for YHWH without waiting on Him:

1. We lose the urgency of prayer just when we need it most.

2. We cannot stay in touch with YHWH whenever He hides His face from us.

3. We are exposed to the power of our own sin.

We can only imagine the devastating amount of negative effect these three results have on any anointing YHWH has planned for our work.

We need a waiting attitude of sufficient influence in us that will alter of ministry motivations and remove this barrier to His presence (anointing).

Third - Stop working for YHWH without His covering (Tallit or Chupah) over our lives.

We see no scriptural evidence for man's covering as is so popular in these times. The scriptures speak much more of mutual submission than some hierarchy of power and authority.

The ascension gifts mentioned in Ephesians 4:11 are not titles nor are they authorities to be used to suppress believer's missions or to oppress ministries with dictatorial attitudes and practices.

Rabbi Shaul says in Ephesians 2:20 that the Apostles and Prophets are to function as a foundation for believer's ministries joined to Yeshua as the Chief Cornerstone.

This is not a top down corporate style hierarchy so commonly practiced in religious systems.

YHWH is Head of His Body. He is the covering over all believers and ministries. Our accountability ought to be mutual and respectful recognizing YHWH's callings and gifts in one another's lives.

When Moses went up Mt. Sinai he met with YHWH under a "covering cloud (cf. Exodus 24:15)." The Hebrew language implies a *chupah* under which the Israelites would marry.

The Torah Moses received is the *ketubah* (marriage covenant) written by the "finger of YHWH" and YHWH marries all of Israel under the covering cloud or the *chupah*.

Remember when Yeshua called out to Jerusalem in Matthew 23:37, *"Jerusalem, Jerusalem, killing the prophets and stoning those who are sent to her! How often I wished to gather your children together, the way a hen gathers her chickens under her wings, but you would not!"*

Another word for "wings" is the *tallit*, or *the hem of the garment.* At the close of a Hebrew service, a father would gather his family under his tallit for the final prayers. This is the picture Yeshua is presenting to Israel.

"He covers with His feathers, and under His wings you take refuge; His truth is a shield and armour." Psalm 91:4

Again, His tallit is our covering even for refuge from danger.

Do we believe some stewards possess varying degrees of authority? Yes, absolutely! But authority is never an oppressive attribute in the Kingdom of YHWH. It is a servant privilege with great responsibility requiring great humility.

Rabbi Shaul writes in Romans 13:8, *"Owe no one any matter except to love one another, for he who loves another has fulfilled the Torah."*

If you are submitted to someone in ministry, do it as unto Yeshua, not out of fear or compulsion. But remember everyone will answer for their own attitudes and efforts regardless of our "covering."

One of the gifts of the Ruach HaKodesh is to be in us and also on us.

"And I shall ask the Father, and He shall give you another Helper, to stay with you forever – the Spirit of Truth, whom the world is unable to receive, because it does not see Him or know Him. But you know Him, for He stays with you and shall be in you." John 15:16-17

There are many barriers to YHWH's presence (anointing), each one diminishing the fullness of His dynamic presence in our lives and upon our stewardship. Every barrier will have to confronted, examined, and eliminated from our think and practice.

If we begin to listen to YHWH, wait upon YHWH, and restore His covering over our lives, significant changes will occur. YHWH is able to do a quick work in us when we are open, humble, and submitted to His presence in our lives.

Now we will learn how to confront strongholds in our lives and communities

The Dance

Chapter Seven

Breaking Strongholds

"For though we walk in the flesh, we do not fight according to the flesh.

For the weapons we fight with are not fleshly but mighty in Elohim for overthrowing strongholds, overthrowing reasonings and every high matter that exalts itself against the knowledge of Elohim, taking captive every thought to make it obedient to the Messiah, and being ready to punish all disobedience, when your obedience is complete." *2 Corinthians 10:3-6*

When we speak of healing the land, we are speaking of land that has been given to our enemy through sin and disobedience. As we wrote earlier, when ground is given to Satan, he builds something on it. What he constructs on surrendered ground is called a stronghold.

A stronghold in Hebrew is *mawoze* meaning "a fortified place," and "a defence." In the Greek language it is *ochuroma* which means to "fortify by holding safely."

For believers it could be stated this way: **a stronghold is the fortification around and the defense of what one believes-especially when one is wrong or deceived.**

<u>Strongholds are erected to protect unmet needs, wounds, fears, and humiliating memories.</u>

Positive strongholds exist also and ought to be constructed by stewards. Whenever a negative stronghold is broken, a positive one should immediately be erected in its place.

Read these two lists of negative and positive strongholds and not how one could replace the other in people's lives:

negative strongholds-------positive stronghold

negative strongholds	positive stronghold
1. Doubt	1. Trust and faith in YHWH
2. Independence	2.Dependence on YHWH
3. False security	3.True security in the Messiah
4. Confusion	4.Understanding reality
5. Un-forgiveness	5.Forgiveness and freedom
6. Distrust	6.Loyalty and trust
7. Control/manipulation	7.Yieldeness and gentleness
8. Self-indulgence	8.Servanthood and stewardship
9. Fear	9.Resolution of anxieties
10. Denial	10.Acknowledgment of existing strongholds

It is easy to observe negative strongholds in others, but it is much more difficult to suggest what positive strongholds could adequately and safely replace the negative ones. We, generally speaking, see "stuff" on others that simply reflect what we don't appreciate about ourselves. Others become a mirror of our own preferences, prejudices, and weaknesses. Looking for the good in others is a rare trait, even for believers. If you spot it, you got it.

If we would not think or speak negatively about others without including positive alternatives about them, we would find ourselves less judgmental and more at peace. We need to give others the space and tolerance they require to " work out their own salvation in fear and trembling (Phil.2:12)."

Not everyone has to learn things the hard way like us – right?

The strongholds Satan builds are in the minds and thinking of the people living on the land. We know of large areas where people live in fear because the stronghold called superstition was erected there.

Strongholds become foundational thinking patterns in people's minds leading to distorted and dysfunctional behaviors. For instance:

Something traumatic occurs (abuse, injury, etc.) in one's life which leads to developing a wrong pattern of thinking, which helps them justify a wrong behavior, which causes one to erect a stronghold to protect one's right to do so – which perpetuates the pain by holding the trauma locked in and YHWH's delivering salvation out.

It's not difficult to realize how Satan capitalizes on such kinds of attitudes and actions, causing the land to become increasingly defiled by the sins of an active and persistent stronghold.

"The one who keeps on sinning is of the devil, because the devil has sinned from the beginning. For this purpose the Son of Elohim was manifested: to destroy the works of the devil." 1 John 3:8

"Yet thus said YHWH , "Even the captives of the mighty is taken away, and the prey of the ruthless is delivered; and I strive with him who strives with you, and I save your children." Isaiah 49:25

These are powerful scriptures about breaking the strongholds over our lives.

Every stronghold includes an identifiable strongman that must be bound and his power expelled, his influence renounced, and a love for that stronghold broken for freedom to commence.

People can actually fall in love with their stronghold because their identity has become identified with that stronghold. Their behavioral habits have become their character, thus becoming their identity. Fear will not allow them to replace the negative stronghold with a positive one without losing their identity. People's lives become an endeavor in acting and pretense to secure one's familiar identity.

In the movie, Smoke Signals, the actors ask this question of one another, "What will happen to us if we forgive our fathers?" "Who will we be?"

Their identity had become saturated with bitterness and unforgiveness – an actual stronghold.

YHWH has a new, better, and more powerful identity He wants to gift every one of us. He wants to make us "new creatures in Messiah."

We don't lose our essential identity – our dysfunctional one is redeemed and restored to a new functional life.

"And if I, by Be'elzebul, do cast out demons, by whom do your sons cast them out? Because of this they shall be your judges. But if I cast out demons by the Spirit of Elohim, then the reign of Elohim has come upon you. Or how is one able to enter a strong man's house and plunder his goods, unless he first binds the strong man? And then he shall plunder his house." Matthew 12:27-29

First, bind the strongman. Identify him. Pray, fast, discern, counsel, think, research, and examine all evidence until he is identified. Be careful, as he will try to mask himself as something acceptable or, worse yet, even necessary for your life.

Don't be deceived by his word games and deceit. Bind him with strong cords of faith, the Torah of YHWH, and the sacrifice of Yeshua the Messiah.

Second, loose his hold on stolen possessions; emotions, relationships, expressions of faith, wealth, intellect, freedoms, and destiny. He will attempt to make you think he owns these Creator given possessions. He is a liar, thief, and destroyer.

Third, make room in your life to receive back the stolen goods. Room must be made for restoration or we will squander our opportunities.

Both negative and positive strongholds need to be submitted to the control of YHWH's Ruach HaKodesh. We can't afford to allow any victories to become evidences of righteousness of our own making. Whatever strongholds YHWH establishes in and through us are opportunities for humble stewardship and not self-righteousness.

"You do not make for yourself a carved image, or any likeness of that which is in the heavens above, or which is in the earth beneath, or which is in the waters under the earth, you do not bow down to them nor serve them. For I, YHWH your Elohim am a jealous El, visiting the crookedness of the fathers on the children to the third and fourth

generations of those who hate Me, but showing kindness to thousands, to those who love Me and guard My commands."

Exodus 20:4-6

YHWH instructs us about generational strongholds. He tells us that sin has both a history and a heritage. It leaves a legacy which us usually dismal at best, and at worst, deadly.

But the sins of our forefathers do not have to rule or reign over our lives and families. Generational curses can be bound and broken, the strongholds dismantled and a new lineage of righteousness begun.

Ancestral patterns of un-forgiveness, addiction, lying, violence, divorce, abuse, anger, suicide, and incest can influence succeeding generations. They are not absolute causes of sin but their influence is formidable and stands as an open door to evil opportunities. Every generation commits its own sin.

A person is not as shaped by the environment as much as he/she is by their perception of the environment. It's not the events in life themselves but how we interpret them that set up the thinking and behavioral patterns in our lives. One tendency is to think that certain events or activities determine how we act or feel. Those events or activities may have a strong influence, but we choose our responses in life, they are not made for us by outside sources.

YHWH created us as sentient beings, meaning we have the power of choice. He honors our choices, although He can and does strongly influence them towards His instructions (Torah). He will not make choices on our behalf except in those areas where we are totally surrendered to His will and purpose in our lives. Even then we must choose to cooperate or not.

If what we believe does not reflect the truth, then what we feel does not reflect reality.

Here are some **internal influences** – not causes:

1. Wrong attitudes
2. Wrong thinking patterns
3. Wrong beliefs
4. Wrong ideas (superstitions)
5. Wrong desires
6. Wrong behaviors
7. Wrong habits

Here are **external influences** – not causes:

1. Word curses
2. Generational strongholds
3. Family and friends
4. Neighborhood, work, and worship environments
5. Local, national, and international events

Influence is not cause. Both YHWH and Satan are influential in our lives but they honor our created ability to choose. Our freedoms are in the choosing.

Healing, deliverance, cleansing, and repentance – these are all choices we make. Thank YHWH He has given us ability to choose.

Remember, **the Ruach HaKodesh will ALWAYS lead or influence us toward obedience, never toward disobedience.**

The Scriptures refer to curses 230 times and names 70 specific sins that foment curses.

"I have called the heavens and the earth as witnesses today against you: I have set before you life and death, the blessing and the curse. Therefore you shall choose life, so that you live, both you and your seed, to love YHWH, your Elohim, to obey His voice, and to cling

to Him – for He is your life and the length of your days – to dwell in the land which YHWH swore to your fathers, to Abraham, to Isaac, and to Jacob, to give them." *Deuteronomy 30:19-20*

Every individual chooses for him/herself whether to be blessed or cursed.

We can determine if a curse rests upon our lives and why (see chapter on spiritual mapping). Yeshua's redemptive provisions of the cross can propel us from curse to blessing. Here are some helpful steps to consider:

1. **Affirm your testimony** – Revelation 12:11
   "And they overcame him (the devil) because of the Blood of the Lamb (His provisions of the cross), and because of the Word of their witness (testimony), and they did not love their lives to the death (see testimony of Cassie Bernall-Spiritual mapping chapter)."

We are overcomers by the "word of our testimony" which means we can affirm our relationship with our Creator by recounting the blessing of His works in our lives.

"And by this we know that we are of the truth, and shall set our hearts at rest before Him, that if our hearts condemns us, Elohim is greater than our heart, and knows all." 1 John 3:19-20

Satan is an accuser and is constantly accusing us before YHWH, but we overcome him by affirming our testimony before YHWH and the world.

2. **Repent of all known sin** – 1 John 2:1-2
   "My little children, I write this to you, so that you do not sin. And if anyone sins, we have an Intercessor with the Father, Yeshua Messiah, a righteous One. And He Himself is an atoning offering for our sins, and not for our sins only but also for all the world."

Repentance in Hebrew is *shoov*, a *shin* and a *beit,* which means "destroy the house." It is similar to the American idiom "burning your bridges behind you." It means to eliminate all the previous options and return to His covenant relationship. In fact if one adds the Hebrew letter *Tav* to *shoov* you arrive at *shabat* – the *tav* is the letter for cross, mark, sign, or covenant. If someone repents (teshuva) and returns to the covenant, they experience *shabat* or *rest*. *Shabat* is not merely the form of 24 hours of not working, it is the function of repentance and returning to YHWH's covenant, then, and only then, will we experience **REST.**

Repentance commences with admitting our sins are wrong. One of my ministry friends used to say, "The conviction of Ruach HaKodesh is agreeing with Him against ourselves." What an excellent way of stating the obvious!

Repentance is admitting our sins were wrong, asking forgiveness for them including making amends, and committing our thinking to not repeating them.

Repentance is always a gift of grace. It's a gift because our thinking is distorted and we do not readily recognize how wrong we've been toward YHWH and others.

3. **Renounce generational curses** – Exodus 20:5-6

Both the accounts of Nehemiah and Ezra testify of people repenting for the sins of their forefathers to break the generational curses over their people.

If spiritual mapping can have been done so specific sins can be renounced, so much the better. Ruach HaKodesh is able to reveal history at any time through His gift of Word of Knowledge.

Renouncing a specific sin means to surrender it voluntarily, not clinging to its enticing effects. In others words, we must not make a "baby blankie" out of past sins because we find some security or identity in them. We must renounce every curse of which we are made aware.

4. **Accept YHWH's forgiveness** – 1 John 1:9

"If we confess our sins, He is trustworthy and righteous to forgive us the sins and cleanse us from all unrighteousness."

YHWH does not hold grudges against His repentant stewards. He desires us to be free, more than we want to be free. Many believers are actually afraid of freedom because of the accountability implicit in it.

YHWH's functions through Yeshua the Messiah in His death and resurrection were to purchase complete freedom for us in this life and the next. Not to accept YHWH's forgiveness is to place one's own feelings above His actual work of redemption.

"In the freedom with which Messiah has made us free, stand firm, then, and do not again be held with a yoke of slavery." Galatians 5:1

5. **Forgive those who have sinned against you** – Luke 6:36-37

"Therefore be compassionate, as your Father also is compassionate. And do not judge, and you shall not be judged at all. Condemn not, and you shall not be condemned at all. Forgive, and you shall be forgiven."

Un-forgiveness and bitterness are in themselves forms of curses. People are going to disappoint, hurt, and sin against us – that's life. People fail others and themselves.

Become a forgiving person and allow the Ruach HaKodesh to confront other people and their attitudes or actions. Don't allow other people's wrongs against you to become a burden or a hindrance to healing the land. Remain as free as the Messiah has made you.

6. **Renounce contact with the enemy** – Luke 6:43-45

"For a good tree does not yield rotten fruit, nor does a rotten tree yield good fruit. For each tree is known by its own fruit. For they do not gather figs from thorns, nor do they gather grapes from a bramble bush. The good man brings forth what is good out of the good treasure of his heart, and the wicked man brings what is wicked out of the wicked treasure of his heart. For out of the overflow of the heart (mind) his mouth speaks."

Some people practice syncretism, which is to combine local or personal religious beliefs with biblical faith, creating a new system of religious belief (see Dr. Richard Twiss' article in the appendix). Many people continue to practice some form of superstition which mixes faith making room for the enemy.

Some religious systems forbade certain cultural practices out of a mono-cultural worldview although the scriptures held no injunction against such practices (i.e. drumming, dancing, regalia, etc.). Some system's taboos' can become another form of legalism. Continue in the grace of YHWH at all times.

If you have experimented in the cults or other forms of idolatry, renounce them completely, confess them, and live a different life.

7. **Cast out all demons of curse** – Matthew 12:43-45

"Now when the unclean spirit goes out of a man, he goes through dry places, seeking rest, and finds none. Then it says, 'I shall return to my house from which I came.' And when it comes, it finds it empty, swept, and decorated. Then it goes and takes with it seven other spirits more wicked than itself, and they enter and dwell there. And the last of that man is worse than the first. So shall it also be with this wicked generation."

Where specific demonic influence can be identified, break that power using the Name Yeshua HaMeshiach of Nazareth. Where a specific demonic influence is unknown, identify the curse as diligently as possible and break its power.

Some stewards are endowed with a gift called "discerning of spirit" and they may need to be consulted to help procure the desired freedom.

YHWH does not lead us into any bondage but is always encouraging true freedom, not license, and blessings.

"For I know the plans I have for you, says Adonai, 'plans for well-being and not for trouble, to give you a future and a hope." Jeremiah 29:11 New Life

YHWH is willing and capable of helping us to destroy the strongholds in our lives and communities. He wants to heal the land and prepare the earth for the reign of Yeshua.

Chapter Eight

Indigenous Peoples

"And He has made from one blood every nation of men to dwell on all the face of the earth, having ordained beforehand the times and the boundaries of their dwelling, to seek the Master, if at least they would reach out for Him and find Him, though He is not far from each one of us."

Acts 17:26-27

Indigenous people, wherever they are found, are not where they are by accident or chance, but by Divine design, purpose, and forethought. The Creator endowed the First Nations people (indigenous people) with the stewardship authority over the lands where He placed them.

Don't forget there's a difference between ownership and stewardship. YHWH will always remain the Owner of His universe and, thus He has the right to place people groups according to His own purposes (see Psalm 24:1).

In stewardship of the land, however, arises both opportunity and responsibility to cleanse, redeem, and heal the land. Both indigenous people and their cultures must experience redemption for this stewardship to be manifested in the earth.

From the program brochure of the World Christian Gathering on Indigenous Peoples held is Rapid City, South Dakota in 1998, is this article, titled *The Way of Things:*

In Indigenous/Native cultures we have a way of looking at life. Underlying this view is an awareness of God's sovereignty. Many of our expressions looked on the work of his hands and said, "It is good."

But first man and woman became deceived in their own eyes, and their hearts were darkened by pride. They said to themselves they could make their own decisions and didn't need to listen to what Creator has asked them both to do and not do. They walked away from Him in their thinking because they felt just as wise as Creator.

Wind Swept
Suuqiina

This broke the heart of their heavenly Father. He had created them in His own likeness and image to know Him, talk with Him, and walk in His ways. Yet they walked away. People have been following other ways ever since.

Because of their rebellion, the Creator hid His face from them. They could no longer know Him face to face. Instead, He only let them see His reflection through the earth, the sky and living things. But Himself, He kept hid from them.

From that time until now people have been lost. They have been searching for the way back home, looking for a way back to harmony with their heavenly Father, their Creator.

First man and woman sent all their children, grandchildren and every generation after them, down a trail leading away from YHWH. Today the Creator is hidden to all human beings all over the face of the earth. The black man, white man, yellow man and red man all have the same "lostness" problem.

In a futile attempt to find their way back home, every tribe or nation has created their own gods and developed religions to make or earn their way back. Many tribes around the world worship some part of creation thinking it is the Creator. Mountains, animals, the sun, even life itself, are worshipped and consulted, as well as many kinds of spirits by people searching for the way home. The spiritual condition of religious men and women in every nation is still the same....lost.

The Creator knew that first man and woman would turn from and reject Him, and lose their way. Because He loves His children so much, He made a way for them to find their way back to Him. He has once again revealed His face to us so we can know Him and talk to Him and walk in His ways.

YHWH is holy and pure and is only sacred, while human beings are unclean and have evil in their hearts. The darkness of people's minds and the uncleanness and rebellion of men's hearts keep them at a great distance from their Creator. YHWH calls this condition of people's hearts, "missing the mark" or sin.

Our heavenly Father has given an invitation for all His children to come home. He has said He will wipe away all the pain and tears of the past and make everything new again. He is inviting you to enjoy a loving relationship with Him in a heart-to-heart, face-to-face way as His son or daughter.

He sent His Son to take your place and pay the price of the death penalty that your sinful condition would have brought upon you. He has bought your life at the cost of His Son Who is the sacrifice for all people's sin everywhere.

This new life is a free gift to you. You only need to accept it to possess it. By faith, trusting in YHWH's love and forgiveness, you can receive Yeshua the Messiah as the One who saves you, and then trust your heart and life to His love and care.

No tribal ceremony can ever remove the guilt and darkness of the human heart. Only Yeshua the Messiah, through the "one for all ceremony," which is His death on a cross, resurrection from the dead, and ascension back into heaven, can you find peace and freedom to live a good life on this earth.

Yeshua is a brown-skinned, dark-haired tribal man – not a white man. His plan and purpose for all people is not the religion of those of white European ancestry. He did not come to condemn our indigenous/native cultures, but to make them all he intended for them to be from the beginning – to fulfill the longing in our hearts.

You can take a minute to pray and accept Yeshua the Messiah into your life right now. If you pray this prayer, you will know what it means to once again, find the path of beauty.

You will have the power and understanding to see and live in a whole new way. This is the promise of a loving YHWH Who promises His children a new and abundant life.

You will know the Creator as the Lakota people call Him, Ate Wakan Tanka, "Heavenly Father."

After you have prayed, tell a believing friend or acquaintance about decision and prayer. Now enjoy all the good promises that YHWH has for His children everywhere!"

Rev. Billy Graham said at a prayer breakfast, *"The greatest moments of Native History may lie ahead of us if a great spiritual renewal and awakening should take place. The Native American has been sleeping giant. He is awakening. The original Americans could become the evangelists who help win America for Christ! Remember these forgotten people!"*

Here is a prophetic word from a man who sees indigenous peoples with a future and a destiny.

We don't believe YHWH has ever forgotten us, but rather the dominant cultures have ignored and dismissed us as irrelevant. We have been kept hidden until these last days. We've been reserved, pun intended, until these times.

Indigenous people must invest their time in learning about who they are and why they are here. They must understand why YHWH wants to restore their dances, drums, regalia, languages, and cultural practices as a means to reach the nations.

In one of President Kennedy's addresses he said, *"It seems a basic requirement to study the history of our Indian people. America has much to learn about the heritage of our American Indians. Only through this study can we as a nation do what must be done if our treatment of the American Indian is not to be marked down for all time as a national disgrace."*

Most of us haven't understood the history of Indigenous Peoples and, thus we haven't understood their potential contribution to the majority culture or to the Body of Messiah.

If something or someone is perceived as important, it or they can be assigned with value. If something has value, it becomes needed and sometimes necessary for life. Most needed things also become desirable things. They become things sought for and obtained at considerable cost.

The Indigenous People have never been viewed as important to the contemporary life of our nation; thus we have no perceived value. Without value we are unneeded, and in most cases unnecessary. As has been often mentioned amongst native people, "Why are we loved in every nation of the world but one – our own?"

YHWH is redeeming the cultures for at least two reasons: Because He wants to, and so that Indigenous People can worship Him in "Spirit and in truth," using the cultural gifts He placed in them including their dances, languages, drums, regalia, stories, etc.

Of course, not everyone agrees with these statements, certainly many of the European immigrants didn't agree. Note:

"With his fall the nobility of the Redskin is extinguished, and what are left as a pack of whining curs who lick the hand that smites them. The whites, by law of conquest, by justice of civilization, are master of the American continent, and the best safety of the frontier settlements will be secured by the total annihilation of the few remaining Indians."

L. Frank Baum, author of the *Wizard of Oz*

Unfortunately, the United State Congress believed in Mr. Baum's philosophy and began "gifting" the Indian, Inuit, and Hispanic native tribal settlements with small pox infected blankets. These had the desired effect and the fact that some of us survived was a miracle of our Creator.

When the first religious missionaries arrived, they brought a form of the gospel, including two ethnocentric preferences:

1. Indigenous peoples should (and would) adopt European forms of religious practice, music styles and instruments, and "appropriate" appearance.
2. Indigenous peoples must reject their own culture, including, language, regalia, musical styles and instruments, and their expressive dances.

While indigenous peoples are deeply indebted to Europeans for bringing them the gospel about YHWH, Europeans did not bring YHWH with them. He has never abandoned His land, anywhere. Many missionaries did not bring a gospel of truth but rather a European religious system rooted in mono-culturalism.

YHWH had lovingly revealed Himself to indigenous peoples long ago. That revelation had been rejected in favor of shamanism and animism. A majority of indigenous people groups retain stories of creation, the great flood, A Father/Son Creator, and the "tree of life." YHWH has deposited the general revelation of Himself in all tribes of the earth, trusting they would seek after Him and find Him.

Sometimes First Nation peoples accuse one another of accepting the "white man's God," while ignoring a multitude of native prophets YHWH used to foretell the arrival of the "rest of the story."

The gospel is not the story, it's the "rest of the story." The story was begun by YHWH in His general revelation to all people.

Ninety miles northwest of Nome, Alaska, is the island known as King Island. Known as Ooq-vok ("a place for winter") by the Inuit; it was inhabited by them because to the abundant resources there. There migrations of walruses, whales, seals, and many kinds of fish. Birds nested there and berries were abundant. The island, mostly rock with sheer cliffs, provided a natural barrier to attack from enemies. These are the ancestors of my heritage, my family and tribal heritage.

Paul Tiulana is one of the traditional Chiefs of King Island. He was born there in the early 1920's, before contact with the white man. He was named "Tiulana" after his grandfather. His "Christian" name, "Paul," came later, when he was baptized by a priest. This priest brought "Christ the King" to the island, which was a statue of Jesus wearing a King's crown. The Inuit labored with ropes and tackle to place the statue atop the island.

Tiulana explains in Inuit terms, the coming of white men, and how "Christ the King" chased away a demon who lived on the other side of the Island.

"The statue was immediately accepted by the Inuit because, ten years earlier, an elder had dreamed, prophetically, about it. The elder said, "An ivuksuk (white man) would come and add to their faith and bring a shiny, silver thing to the island."

Another elder told Tiulana about a medicine man who said the universe had a Creator. He said, "If you eat the flesh and drink the blood of the Universes Creator, you will be safe and live forever." This was before anyone of King Island had heard the "rest of the story." (Shannon Lowry, *Natives of the Far North*)

In the Kobuk River area of the Northwest Alaska Region known as NANA, the history and stories of the Inuit prophet Maniilaq (Man-nee-luk) are well known.

Although he lived and prophesied in the mid-eighteen hundreds, Maniilaq told of the coming of the white man, and that the white man would bring light in the form of a black book. He also prophesied power boats, airplanes, heat stoves, telephones, the overthrow of shamanism, and many end-time events with great detail. He told of the return of the Creator's Son and declared it would in this present time, the life-time of his great-grandchildren, who are alive at this time. He introduced Sabbath worship and rest to the Inuit people. He would prophecy with song and drumming. He had great visions and would laugh at the taboos of the shamans often deliberately breaking the taboos to eliminate superstition from the people's thinking. He remains a revered indigenous prophet to this day.

These indigenous prophets, along with many others (Chief Seattle, Chief Black Elk, Chief Tecumseh, etc.), show us how YHWH was preparing the indigenous nations for the arrival of the "rest of the story." Most tribes have redemptive analogies built into their culture, ie. accounts of creation, memories of a great flood, a tree of life pole or post, prophecies, art and music that speak of the general revelation YHWH placed within the tribes to entice them to seek Him "although He is not far from any (Acts 17:27)."

The first missionary to visit New Zealand was gifted by the Maori with a statute of a woman holding an infant. The infant's face was covered with moko (facial tattoos) indicating he had more authority than anyone in the tribe. He was sticking out his tongue in defiance of death. The missionary priest viewed the statute as somehow demonic and put it away for many years. This Maori art could have been used as a bridge to the people; the infant represents Yeshua who has more authority than anyone in the tribe and was born defying death.

Images of King Island and the village of Ukivok.

Current missionary worldviews are changing to include understanding the cultures of the gospel recipients, their art, language, dance, music and regalia. These cultural elements are now being viewed as bridges to the people's hearts. The stories and prophetic evidences amongst the tribes are being acknowledged as significant.

YHWH is again seeking for indigenous prophets who will stand and speak for Him and for their people. You may be one of them.

In the Book of Acts, chapter 10:1-48, is the account of the conversion of Cornelius, a non-Jew. Peter, a Jew and disciple of Yeshua, is sent to perform cross-cultural ministry and not thrilled with the idea. He was, at the time, mono-cultural in his thinking. He has forgotten that YHWH intended to save all nations and not just one.

The Greeks, Cornelius' people, were steeped in idolatry and sin. But the Jews were also so steeped in sin they had rejected the presence of their Messiah. In this account, it must be noted that **YHWH did not require Cornelius to abandon his sin-stained culture and embrace the sin-stained culture of the Jews.**

Ask yourself, "Can I be an American and a believer?" Of course. Now ask, "Can I be Native and a believer?" Many times the answer has been a resounding, "No!" We were allowed to be Natives OR believers.

The Indigenous Peoples of any cultures shouldn't have to abandon their identities to receive the "rest of the story." No one should be forced to adopt someone else's cultural expressions as their own for their salvation to be perceived as having integrity.

Modern missions' movements have much to repent for in stripping Indigenous Peoples of their essential identity before their Creator.

A huge portion of every culture is redeemable and useful for enhancing the varieties in the Body of Messiah. The Apostle John saw "Every tribe, heard every language, and observed every nation at YHWH's throne (see Revelation 7:9)."

When the Chief Dancer commanded His people to dance (see Psalm 149:3; 150;4, etc.), He was not telling all the peoples of the earth to dance like the Jews, using their rhythms, their instruments, their musical scale or their regalia. What He is telling all peoples everywhere, YHWH is worthy of our hands and feet, indeed our whole bodies, for expressions in worship to Him.

Some used their dances to worship Satan or demons, but it was their allegiance that was in error, not the dance. Instruments such as the native drum, trap sets, or congas' do not know if they are being played by a believer or a shaman, nor do they really care. The real issue is the allegiance of the drummer's heart.

Indigenous People must reclaim the redeemable aspects of their cultures for the glory and honor of the Creator.

"I said that most non-Indians have not been able to discern value in Native cultural expressions of Christianity and therefore do not see their own need to include these Native expressions with their own."

Dr. Richard Twiss, *Culture and Christianity, a seminar teaching.*

We are not saying that Native drums are better than other drums, or that our dance expressions are better than other dances, but our expressions are certainly not "less-than" other expressions. They are not demonic, evil, or wicked.

It is time for Indigenous Peoples around the world to bring forth with anointed words in poetry, music, dance and stories, using their own cultural expressions with freedom, dignity, honor, and beauty.

We continue to ask the Euro-American majority church to make room in their hearts to be accepting of our expressions, without feeling pressure to have to adopt them. There is enough room in the Body of Messiah for every expression of true worship to YHWH.

True, anointed, culturally accepted worship will contribute, in a huge way, to the healing of the land. Along with repentance for past wrongs done to Indigenous Peoples, restoration and acceptance of their cultural identities must be included for renewal to visit our land.

Repentance must go both directions. Many Indigenous Peoples harbor reverse prejudices and feel justified in acting upon them with their attitudes and actions toward others. Reconciliation is never a one-way street.

Pointing fingers at one another accomplishes nothing, in fact, Satan would delight in having us continue that forever. Repentance, reconciliation, restoration, and relationship are all partnership realities that require both parties to participate. We need one another!

"The absence of Christian Native leaders in key leadership roles in the evangelical mainstream in America today is an accurate indicator that Native American believers have never been recognized as having anything of value to contribute to the Body of Christ.

Doesn't it seem reasonable to think that after four to five hundred years of steady evangelism at least two or three Native Americans would have emerged as significant leaders in contemporary American evangelicalism?" ibid., Dr. Twiss

First Nations believers must begin to believe that YHWH is preparing them for participation in the harvest fields of the world. We must prepare ourselves as Indigenous people to be one of the people YHWH can use in these times.

We need to tune up our instruments, practice our dance steps, learn our stories, and ready our regalia for assignments that lie ahead.

Because of Hollywood's portrayal of Native Americans, we have been popularized all over the globe. Everywhere, the American Indian is thought of as unique and special amongst the nations of the world. We need to see this as YHWH's opportunity to use us. The way has been prepared for us by an industry that did little to honor us or our ways. A prepared way is much, much better than no way.

It is time for the majority church to realize that Indigenous Peoples aren't merely the mission field, but they are themselves missionaries capable of bringing the "rest of the story" to others. YHWH has positioned Indigenous Peoples to reach other nations for many reasons, including but not limited to, similar histories, tribal values, appreciation for ceremony, pride of identity, and a universal desire to heal the land.

When people prayer-walk or speak to the earth in their communities, it is of vital importance they include First Nations representatives from that area. They carry a unique authority, gifting, and expression of intercession necessary for healing the land. You'll be glad you included them, and they will be delighted to fulfill their role in the Body of Messiah. Please do not use natives for spiritual purposes and then discard them. That is exploitation and it is demeaning, dishonoring, and defiling.

For a vast majority of Indigenous Peoples, the issues are not land, money, or welfare. The issues are focused on regaining respect and restoring dignity.

Indigenous People have a land stewardship that is necessary and important for healing the land. It needs to be recognized and appreciated.

It seems that ethnic cleansing is a generational curse that revisits the nations on a regular schedule. It is a demonic spirit. It is vulgar, wicked, mean, and hateful. It is an abomination in YHWH's sight.

It, however, doesn't always manifest itself as military action or terrorism. Sometimes it is limited to attitudes and verbal expressions designed to the kill the spirit of a people group. Note these recent expressions about the Makah (Northwest Washington) tribe, who successfully hunted a whale:

"So hostile has been the protest to the hunt that Makah tribe members have put their reservation, inundated with death threats, in a state of war-time alert. Bomb threats have evacuated Indian schools."

(Local newspaper article.)

The article continues, "The Makahs have been called savages, drunkards, and laggard. Protestors have entreated people to "Save a whale, harpoon a Makah." Calls for a return to killing Indians like in the Old Wild West have appeared on Internet chat rooms and in newsletters."

Ernie D., Everett, WA' "(to the Makahs) Maybe you can try just as hard at getting an education as you did training for the kill. Why don't you start a new tradition: take pride in yourselves..and work for a living instead of finding your courage in the death of a defenseless mammal or at the bottom of a bottle?"

Mark M., Redmond,WA: "I have a very real hatred for Native Americans now. It's embarrassing, but I would be lying if I said it wasn't the truth."

Wendy and Erica (mother and daughter), Seattle, WA: "Hey, I think we should also be able to take their land if they can take our whales. Publish this article but don't use our last names. We wouldn't want to lose our scalps."

Phillip W., Pebble Beach, CA: "I am anxious to know where I may apply for a license to kill Indians. My forefathers helped settle the West and it was their tradition to kill every redskin they saw. 'The only good Indian is a dead Indian,' they believed. I also want to keep faith with my ancestors."

Michael C., Seattle, WA: "They are a modernized welfare race. I personally hate the Makah Tribe. I hope and pray for a terrible end to the Makah Tribe, very slow and very painful."

When we begin to hear words that it is again time to hunt Indians or anyone, we must realize that is the language of genocide. We've never heard that it is time to hunt white men when a couple of drunken white men drag a black man to his death behind a pickup truck. This is the language of hate, arrogance, and prejudice. It is evil to think, much less, speak this way.

This, too often, is the human heart towards people different than our selves. We often encourage ethnic diversity, until the native community does something that doesn't agree with our perception of what others can or cannot do.

The non-native community has demanded that Natives act or live in some manner other than their traditional way. The majority church is not far behind.

Where are the headlines of the majority church standing with the Makah? Where are the editorials in defense of the Makah? Where are the picketers holding signs on behalf of the Makah? Where is the church?

Don't tell anyone that we Alaskans continue to kill and eat whales every year.

Ethnic cleansing occurs in the human heart first. What about the place where you worship. Does it continue to practice ethnic cleansing? It may not be doing it overtly, but is there any evidence of embracing diversity?

I visited a church "for all nations" once whose membership included whites, African American, Native Americans, Asian Americans, Hispanics, and others, however, the worship band consisted only of white people. Did none of the other people groups have enough talent to be included in the band? Why the pretense that this church was for "all nations," when their expression was obviously mono-cultural and designed to exclude diversity?

Indigenous People are being used in mighty ways to expand the horizons of YHWH's Kingdom on earth. Despite centuries of attempts at total annihilation we can say, "We are still here!"

We are here to help heal the land.

Down the Hatch *oil by Suuqiina*

Chapter Nine

To The Nations

What is the ultimate purpose for healing the land? Does it go beyond producing larger and better crops for harvest? Is it simply about our stewardship of the land and its resources? Or does healing the land increase YHWH's Kingdom is some manner?

There are two key purposes for healing the land:

1. **To build relationships** –

"For I am persuaded of this, that He who has begun a good work in you shall perfect it until the day of Yeshua Messiah." *Philippians 1:6*

YHWH imparts knowledge to begin new relationships or to nourish existing ones. Insights, techniques, freedoms, and opportunities are all wonderful, but they have no practical value if relationships aren't improved with YHWH, our families, and our land.

I remember when Ted Turner, the television tycoon, usually an arrogant, overconfident, and boisterous personality was asked by an interviewer if he had any regrets. His answer was, with bowed head and misty eyes, "Yes, how I treated my first Wife." (Larry King show)

It's about relationships and improving them.

Lee Iaccoca, designer of the Ford Mustang, rebuilder of the Crysler Corporation, when asked, "What was the most important thing in the world to him," replied, "My relationship with my family." (Larry King program)

If YHWH were asked what the most important thing in the universe is to Him, He would reply, "My relationship with My family." He wants to improve, enhance, restore, heal, whatever it takes – He's about relationship.

2. **To the nations** –

"And Yeshua came up and spoke to them, saying, 'All authority has been given to Me in heaven and on earth. Therefore, go and make taught ones of all the nations, immersing them in the Name of the Father and of the Son and of the Set-apart Spirit, teaching them to guard all that I have commanded you. And see, I am with you always, until the end of the age." Amen." *Matthew 28:18-20*

Here is the post-resurrection "Great Commission" Yeshua gave all His followers. He anchors the commission in the authority He was given in Heaven and on earth.

In this account by Matthew, Yeshua presents the **mission orientation** of His command; it includes going, discipling, baptizing, and teaching obedience. Along with the job description Yeshua makes this special promise – "I am with you always..."

We've heard many prayers invoking His presence, but here it is unmistakable: His presence is where His followers are when they go to the nations.

"But you shall receive power when the Set-apart Spirit has come upon you, and you shall be My witnesses in Jerusalem, and in all Judea and Samaria, to the ends of the earth." *Acts 1:8*

Here Yeshua gives a **geographic orientation** to His command. He tells us to begin where we are, reach out further, and then to the farthest places on earth.

Some places are difficult to reach merely because of remoteness. There are 29 Inuit tribes in Siberia scattered across 11 time zones. That's the equivalent of traveling from San Francisco to Paris, France. Twenty-seven of these tribes have never heard the "rest of the story." Are they reachable? Absolutely! But it will require obedience and significant personal investment to accomplish it.

We are rapidly concluding the completion of reaching the earth with the gospel.

"This good news about the holy nation of YHWH must be preached over all the earth. It must be told to all nations and then the end will come." *Matthew 24:14 New Life*

You and I are invited to be part of this mission on earth.

"I will keep you safe from the Jews and from the people who are not Jews. I am sending you to these people.

You are to open their eyes. You are to turn them from the power of satan to the power of YHWH. In this way, they may have their sins forgiven. They may have what is given to them, along with all those who are set apart for YHWH by having faith in Me." *Acts 26:17-18*

Here we are presented with a **multi-task orientation** of our great mission. There are **four tasks** with two immediate results:

1. Go to all the nations
2. Open their eyes
3. Turn them from darkness to light
4. Turn them from Satan's power to YHWH's power

Two results –

1. They experience moral freedom, the forgiveness of sins
2. They receive the freedom of stewardship

Task one requires some preparation, probably some education, but mostly a willingness to be available and ready when YHWH sends.

Task two, opening their eyes, requires an eye-opener. YHWH has given every believer a unique eye-opener; his or her testimony. I have heard some powerful, eye-opening testimonies. Every believer has one.

One doesn't have to know very much theology, be excellent at speaking, or have awesome preaching skills, but everyone can share what YHWH has done in their hearts and lives. It will be an eye-opener to someone.

Task three, turning them from darkness to light, requires some effort – good effort.

"Let your light shine in front of men. Then they will see the good things you do and will honor your Father Who is in heaven." *Matthew 5:16*

Don't limit your good works for only believers; save some of them for the pre-believers. Build bridges in their hearts, turning them from darkness to light, using good works, gentle attitudes, and compassionate hearts.

Task four, turning them from Satan's power to YHWH's power, is about demonstrating YHWH's power when He provides opportunities to do so.

Many times our families, friends, or neighbors experience sickness. These are opportunities to demonstrate the mercy of YHWH Rophe in healing power. If there are needs, demonstrate YHWH Yireh's power to provide for us.

We must be willing to demonstrate YHWH's power at these opportunities. We have more power than we can imagine, but we must have faith that YHWH will not disappoint us or let us down.

Pray for and with people; call forth prophetically, manifest words of wisdom or words of knowledge, heal, cast out demons, exhort, encourage, but above all, show compassion. Do not cross personal boundaries or embarrass in any way. It's not about us, it's about YHWH and His love for them.

People really want freedom. They want their eyes opened and they would really appreciate being turned from Satan's power to YHWH's power. Many of them do not understand how this can be accomplished, and they need someone to care enough, to be patient enough, to be kind enough, to help through to freedom. Be willing to hear their story without judging them, their presentation, and do not attempt to justify or defend oppressors.

Thirty years after graduating from high school, I came across a class-mate who asked me, "Why didn't you share Yeshua with me in High School? I was searching for Him and I knew you had the answer." I felt so ashamed and sad for this class-mate. She waited many years before anyone shared Yeshua with her.

YHWH can take us where we cannot take ourselves. Leading lives of worship and intercession can move us from where we are to where YHWH wants us to be. In all of praying, remember to pray for the lost ones.

Our primary mission of stewardship is to sign up every nation in the list of nations to be redeemed (see Revelation 21:24).

As we heal the land, remember why we're doing it. It is so YHWH can bless our land and double His harvest for His great Kingdom.

For the land to be healed, we must move from where we are to the place the Creator has designed for us. This move begins in our hearts. Our minds will need to be renewed so we begin to see the world YHWH does, to see His creatures the way He does, and to see humankind the way He does.

His redemptive work in us is designed to give us hope for eternity, strength for the journey, power for the assigned tasks, equipping for facing the opposition, compassion upon the needy, and success as His stewards of the earth. A true job description!

Get ready...get set...heal the land!

Appendices

A. Blessings of thanks for the earth.

B. Sample prayers over your household.

C. A Warning.

D. Instructions for prayer walking.

E. Excerpts from Culture, Christ, and the Kingdom Seminar
By Dr. Richard Twiss

F. Additional Resources

G. IMI Resources

Appendix A

Blessings of thanks for the earth

These blessings are taken from the Mishnah (Berachot 6,8,and 9), the Babylonian Talmud (Berachot 54a-59b), and the Palestinian Telmud (Berachot 6:1, 9:3).

On tasting fruit for the first time in the season:

Baruch Atah Adonai, Elhoneinu Melch ha-olam, she-he-che-yanu, v'ki-y'manu, v'hi-gianu lazman ha'zeh,

Blessed are You, Lord our God, Ruler of the universe, for giving us life, for sustaining us, and for enabling us to reach this season.

On seeing the beauties of nature:

Baruch Atah Adonai, Eloheinu Melech ha-olam, she-kachah lo b'olamo.

Blessed are You, Lord our God, Ruler of the Universe, whose world is filled with beauty.

On seeing rivers, seas, mountains, and other natural wonders:

Baruch Atah Adonai, Eloheinu melech ha-olam, oseh ma-asey v'reshit.

Blessed are You, Lord our God, Ruler of the universe, who makes the wonders of creation.

On seeing shooting stars, electrical storms, and earthquakes:

Baruch Atah Adonai, Eloheinu Melech ha-olam, she-kocho u'g'vurato maley olam.

Blessed are You, Lord our God, Ruler of the universe, whose power and might pervade the world.

On seeing trees in blossom:

Baruch Atah Adonai, Eloheinu Melech ha-olam, she-lo chiseyr

B'olamo v'ilanot tovim l'ha-not ba-hem davar, u'vara, vo briy,ot tovot b'ney adam.

Blessed are You, Lord our God, Ruler of the universe, whose world lacks nothing needful and who has fashioned goodly creatures and lovely trees that enchant the heart.

On seeing the ocean:

Baruch Atah Adonai, Eloheinu Melech ha-olam, she-asah at ha-yam ha-gadol.

Blessed are You, Lord our God, Ruler of the universe, Make of the great sea.

On seeing a rainbow:

Baruch Atah Adonai, Eloheinu Melech ha-olam, ocher ha-brit, vane-e-man bi'v'rito, b'kayam b'ma-a-maro

Blessed are You, Lord our God, Ruler of the universe, who remembers the covenant with Noah and keeps its promise faithfully with all Creation.

(Ellen Bernstein, *Ecology and the Jewish Spirit, pg.205)*

These are, obviously, Hebrew prayers of thanksgiving for the elements of creation. Maybe you can construct some prayers of thanksgiving for the creation near you. Look for the beauty, wonder, and diversity of the creation near you.

"We must keep alive the sense of wonder through deeds of wonder."

Abraham Joshua Heschel (ibid., Bernstein, pg.200)

Appendix B

A sample prayer over house and property

These prayers include all of the things discussed in this book about healing the land. You can make your own prayers where you live, work, and worship.

If necessary, anoint with oil, touch the walls of your home, mark the boundaries and/or corners of your property, and have family members agree with your prayers – maybe it could be a family project.

Our Father, King of the Universe, Ruler over all, and Creator of all, Your scriptures say, *"The heavens belong to Adonai. But the earth He has given to the children of men."*

Therefore, I accept my responsibility as steward of this land and property. I have authority from Yeshua the Messiah, my Salvation.

I confess _____________ (name sins) which have defiled Your land. This is land I should have protected with my authority and through righteous behaviors. My neglect has offended You and given territory to Satan, placing me, my family, and my household under the effects of oppression, temptation, and curses.

Your scripture reveals, *"If My people who are called by My Name put away their pride and pray, and look for My face, and turn from their sinful ways, then I will hear from heaven. I will forgive their sin, and will heal their land."*

I put away my pride and I look for Your face. I repent of all known sins and will repent for sins you may bring to my attention. I turn away from these sins and I return to Your covenant.

I repent of every attitude that does not reflect Your holy person and every word spoken in a spirit of unjustified anger. I renounce every curse spoken in my house and on this land. I renounce any and all blasphemy of Your holy Name.

I repent of giving land to Satan, and I ask Yeshua the Messiah to restore every piece of it. I repent of the defilements, both ancient and contemporary, by natives and non-natives, including idolatry, immorality, bloodshed, and broken treaties, that were done on this land and property by previous dwellers. I reject all curses or strongholds resulting from their sins, habits, or attitudes.

In the victorious name of Adonai Yeshua the Messiah of Nazareth, I command all evil spirits to depart from this house and property. All encroaching spirits must leave by His powerful name and presence. I break all curses and strongholds established by Satan, and I cover and cleanse this property with the blood of Yeshua that cleanses from all sin. I renounce any and all historical curses and strongholds on this property in the name of Yeshua of Nazareth.

As the scriptures say, *"Son of man, speak in My name to the mountains of Israel, hear the Word of the Lord....So speak about the land of Israel, and tell the mountains, the hills, and valleys...etc."*

Therefore, I speak to this property, telling it of the freedom for which Yeshua the Messiah gave His life.

I commit to the stewardship of this land through regular prayer, diligent gate-keeping, and always ready to repent and return to His covenant. I commit to walk in the truth and to live in agreement with YHWH's holy Torah (Word), in humility and a teachable spirit.

I pray these things and proclaim their truthfulness, receiving the witness of Ruach HaKodesh, of angels, and my household.

This property and home is designed to be a habitation for the presence and power of the living Elohim. You are welcome here, O Holy One of Israel! Aho (Amen)

Appendix C

A Warning

Spiritual warfare is always conducted within the danger zone of Christian systems. Never enter this zone with pride, arrogance, un-confessed sin, or with a religious spirit. You'll find yourself seriously experiencing vengeful attacks.

Healing the land is not a spiritual video game. It's not about power trips or seeing who has the most authority. Some people have been seriously damaged entering this danger zone.

Yes, we can claim YHWH's protection and help, but we must also implicitly obey His Word. Satan and his co-hurts will respond appropriately to YHWH's Word and to His powerful Name.

Do only the things directed by Ruach HeKodesh. Follow His instructions about timing. YHWH has His own calendar and knows the seasons for success. Do the hard work of spiritual mapping. Never assume your present understanding also applies to historical evidence or to future purposes. Be ready and willing to learn new things, gain new understandings, and practice new submissions to proper authorities.

Remember wars are fought by armies, not individuals. Keep a group philosophy and attempt nothing in your own strength alone. Keep His covering and remain mutually accountable in the Body of Messiah.

As much as possible maintain a spirit of humility and shalom (peace). Keep your thinking as clean and clear as is possible. Do not be in a hurry – be patient and allow YHWH to unfold His plan and purpose for healing the land.

Appendix D

Instructions on Mobilizing Prayer Walks

Compiled by Rev. Carl Cady, Prayer Pastor – Door of Hope, Fairbanks, AK

"And the Lord said to Abram...Arise, walk about the land through its length and breadth; for I will give it to you." Genesis 13:17

"Now after this the Lord appointed seventy others, and sent them two and two ahead of Him to every city and place where He Himself was going to come." Luke 10:1

The premise – God does answer prayer; God has a heart for your community, and God can change your city through prayer.

The examples – Abraham was told by the Lord to walk through the land that God would give to him (Genesis 13:17). Caleb was given a similar promise (Deuteronomy 1:36). Caleb and his sons would be given the land that he set his feet upon.

Jesus felt so grieved over the spiritual condition and missed opportunities in Jerusalem that He wept over that city. The Lord saw the city as a mission field.

In Acts 1:8, we are commanded to go first into Jerusalem (our city), all Judea (our region, Samaria (our nation), and even to the remotest part of the earth (our world). We are commanded to begin in our own city.

Jesus sent out seventy men with the assignment to go ahead of Him and walk through each city and test the spiritual hunger of the people, and then either to speak peace, or to shake the dust off their feet if they were hard-hearted and did not receive the men.

The vision – The vision is to unite with Christians in your community to pray for each home, business, public building, and church in your city.

Corporately raise the spiritual openness of the people in your community.

We, as Christ's examples in the community, want to show love for our neighbors by simply praying God's blessing on their lives. This is in accord with the great commandment.

Praying for our neighbors will cause us to see their need with the eyes of Christ.

The strategy – We would suggest that each participant first pray for the neighborhoods where he or she lives. We would suggest each church pray for the neighborhoods that are near them. Keep a map of the city to keep track of the areas that have been prayer walked.

Celebrate with all participating churches the success of the total prayer saturation of your city.

Before you begin – Prepare your heart and mind by spending time in personal prayer. Spend time in God's Word, seeking guidance for everything that will be prayed. Put on the "Armor of God" (Ephesians 6:10-17) and reading Psalm 91. It is best to prayer walk with a partner – this increases faith. Designate the route you plan on walking. Leave your home with prayer on your lips: "Lord, make me instrument of Your love and a blessing to all whom I meet."

During the walk – Make sure God is addressed and people are blessed as you pray. Pray as you walk to "see the city as the Lord would see it" (Ephesians 1:18). Keep your eyes, ears, and heart open as you pray for each home, lot, business, public building, and church. Stop for a moment as you pray at every home and business. Respect property lines and do not trespass. Remember that praying aloud doesn't mean praying loudly. Be open to Bible verses the Lord may give you for the places for which you pray. Pray for each member of the family to come to faith in God. Ask God to release blessing and to bind the efforts of the enemy to deceive and lie to the members of the household. Ask God to reveal every hidden thing and secret thing that has hindered that family from receiving God's love. Some things to remember are: substance abuse, racism, immorality, division, rebellion, loneliness, etc. If you are asked by someone what you are doing, tell them you line in the neighborhood and you are praying for God's love and blessing on each home. (by Rev. Carl Cady)

Note: These instructions came from an evangelical-charismatic source and may not reflect your practices or thinking.

Appendix E

Excerpts from the Culture, Christ, and the Kingdom Seminar

By Dr. Richard Twiss, December 1998

"I humbly offer these perspectives to aid you in your dialogue on culture and Christianity. Like yourself, I am sincerely committed to God's Word in finding Christ-honoring perspectives to some of these difficult questions. Let me make a couple of qualifying statements.

Theologically and doctrinally, I am **adamantly opposed to syncretism** in any form, when it in any way, begins to encroach on the authority of God's Word. And in particular, the work of the cross. Syncretism must be understood as a doctrinal issue, not a socio/cultural one.

I agree fully and completely with the perspective offered by Dr. Chuck Kraft in his book, *Anthropology for Christian Witness*. "We implicitly and explicitly committed ourselves to the Protestant Bible as the revelation of God and, therefore, normative with regard to the understandings we advocate concerning God and His relationship with and desires for humans. He it is who originated, oversees and keeps working all that exists. We see, then, **God as existing above and outside of culture yet working through culture** in His interactions with human beings." (emphasis mine, R.T.)

I also share the concerns expressed by David Hesselgrave and Edward Rommen. They write "Two dangers in approaching the task of contextualization – the fear of irrelevance if contextualization is not attempted, and the fear of compromise and Syncretism if it is taken too far. **There is a need to use existing cultural forms that can be baptized and pressed into the service of Christ if the Gospel is not denied in the process.** (emphasis mine, R.T.) Unless this is done, it is likely that only the surface layers of a culture will be changed. But since by definition contextualization appropriates indigenous linguistic and cultural forms, it always risks cultural and religious Syncretism. **The only viable choice in the face of these two**

dangers is a contextualization that it true to both indigenous culture and the authority of Scripture." (emphasis mine, R.T.) David J. Hesselgrave and Edward Rommen, *Contexualization – Meaning, Methods, and Models* (Grand Rapids, MI; Baker, 1989)pg.55

My aim is to explore biblical approaches and ways to see our cultural forms redeemed and utilized for the cause of Christ and His Kingdom among our people! In my research of missions among Native people in North America, it seems as though for generations the emphasis has been on the fear of potential compromise, often at the gross negligence and expense of the Native people themselves. The result being the relative ineffectiveness of the most powerful message known to humankind to impact Native people.

Repossessing Cultural Forms

Basically, when we speak of redeeming cultural forms we are speaking of redeemed believers in Christ, repossessing those God-given forms that have been erroneously given away or surrendered to ungodly and idolatrous uses and practices. We also mean restoring those cultural expressions that were stripped from us, by an ethnocentric missions mindset. All of this for the singular and sole purpose of restoring them to original intent – praise and worship to Almighty God, through our Lord and Savior Jesus Christ.

For example, can unrighteous mammon – money – be redeemed for the benefit of the Church? Can things formerly used for idolatrous purposes be redeemed or sanctified for God-honoring purposes? Can you name at least five items or cultural forms that are borrowed from other "pagan" cultures that are used every Sunday in the Christian community today?

(see Romans 8:19-22) All of God's creation has an original intent. All things were created by Him and for Him and for His good pleasure they exist (Rev.4:11). God created all things for His glory. In developing a contextualized style of ministry, we are looking to see cultural forms or creation, restored to original intent – praise and worship to Almighty God.

Fallen man uses God's creation or "handiwork" in a misdirected manner in idol worship. Worship involves expressing one's homage, love, fear, adoration, exaltation, etc. to someone or something, through the use of musical instruments, liturgy, chant, singing, dance, art, ceremony – handiwork. Can handiwork, animal hides, wood, stone, plants, etc. used in fashioning drums, traditional dress, some ceremonial objects, artwork, carvings, dance items, be redeemed/repossessed and restored to original intent by Christian people?

We know there are certain forms or practices that cannot be used in any form for Christian worship. This is not an exhaustive list but would include, for example: 1.The prescribed liturgical use of mind-altering substances. 2. Sacrifices of living things and blood sacrifices. 3. Promotion of and participation in sexual immorality. 4. Physical torture and self-abuse. And certainly any practice clearly in opposition to sound biblical doctrine. God's Word in Galatians 5:19-21 gives us a detailed list of activities, attitudes, and sinful behaviors common to all peoples that obviously cannot be pressed into the service of Christ.

Nowhere in the Bible is any musical instrument or style condemned or prohibited for Christian worship. Nor is dance or pageantry. What makes something evil? Can something previously used in an idolatrous manner be sanctified for Christian use? What justifies the type of bongo drums used in voodoo magic in many of our Christian services? How can Messianic Jews use their dancing in Church when Scriptures says they are free from their old ceremonies and laws – religious bondage?

Native Culture Has Value In The Kingdom

Native culture, as all the cultures of man, reflects to some degree the attributes of our Creator Himself. It is in Christ that we find the ultimate fulfillment of His holy and sovereign purpose for us as a people. If He has a unique role for us to play or contribution to make in the fulfilling of His purpose for our nation in these days, then as the Church, we must reconsider the place that we give to the Native expression in the evangelical mainstream in America.

Dr. Chuck Kraft from Fuller Seminary writes, "..we see God working in terms of Jewish culture to reach Jews, yet, refusing to impose Jewish customs on Gentiles. Instead, non-Jews are to come to God and relate to Him in terms of their own cultural vehicles. We see the Bible endorsing, then a doctrine we call *biblical sociocultural adequacy* in which each culture is taken seriously but none advocated exclusively as the only one acceptable to God." (emphasis mine, R.T.) Dr. Charles Kraft, ibid.

Consider these very powerful insights as it applies to Native culture.

"Biblical Christianity is never found apart from a culture. It is always part of a culture. The Christianity of the New Testament was a part of the Greco-Roman world of the 1st century. There is no such thing as plain Christianity. Christianity always expresses itself through a culture. **It is unique in that it can be expressed equally well in any culture."** (emphasis mine, R.T.) (Gunlan & Mayers),pg.230

Sometimes I think many Native Christians believe that we are the only people group in the world who are exempt from this reality. Why are we so distrustful of our cultural identity? Why, as Native Christians, do we believe our drums, music styles, dance and art forms have any less value in the Kingdom than do English hymns, German organs, Welsh choruses, Irish ballads, Italian frescoes and Roman architecture? Why is the use of any of these cultural forms not considered syncretistic when much of it clearly had an ungodly and idolatrous origin?

I believe God gave us our drums, songs, languages, customs, traditions, dances, and beliefs as a way to worship and walk with Him in a way that is beautiful, unique, edifying and ultimately deeply pleasing to Him!

He did not give them to us to frustrate, wound, and embarrass us. As a loving heavenly Father, He did not give us inherently bad or evil things. Regardless of the way that sinful people ended up using drums, ceremony, dance, etc., that fact does not make those things evil or bad, in and of themselves – only misdirected and/or polluted – able to be cleansed.

Whose Culture Most Defines Your Theology?

Cultural worldviews affect the way that people groups interpret and apply God's Word to their respective life experiences. We are naïve if we think our theologies are completely absent and free of our own cultural bias. One author has said there is no such thing as "plain" Christianity, regarding cultural beliefs, expressions and practices, and all missiologists today agree that no theology is free from the influence of the Bible theologian or scholar.

"Naïve idealists reject the notion that their interpretations of scripture are colored by their history or culture, their personal experiences, or even the language they speak. They assume that they understand clearly and without bias what Scripture has to say.

A critical realist approach to theology affirms the priesthood of all believers, and...assumes that all theologies are partial and culturally biased, so that truth in scriptures is greater than our understanding of it. They must see and test one another's theologies and be open to critique." Dr. Paul Heibert, *Anthropological Reflections on Missiological Issues,* (Baker Books, Grand Rapids,MI. 1994) pg.26,30,31

Whose culture has most affected and defined the expression of your Christian faith – Native or Anglo? Is the person of Jesus Christ viewed as being for Native people, while the cultural forms of the church are for white people? Why has our Native culture not been the primary influence in our theologies, when for all European cultures and many tribal peoples in other parts of the world it is? Why do we still believe the influences of Euro-American culture are any less potentially harmful than Native culture?

Walking In The Light and Liberty

Many times I have heard of Christian Native leaders who misinterpret and wrongly apply the scriptures regarding our own culture. They exhort their fellow Native Christians to "come out from among them and be separate" and "touch not the unclean thing" and say "what fellowship does light have with darkness," as if to say our cultures are inherently evil and unclean. I fully acknowledge that there do exist idolatrous and sinful practices that must be repented if, but the Word of God is not calling us to repent or turn away from being who God made us – Native people. To distort the scriptures in such a way is a gross error and rude denial of God's creativity and handiwork in our lives as First Nations people.

When we come to Christ, Jesus does not ask us to abandon one sin-stained culture, only to embrace another sin-stained culture.

John Fisher writes in his book, *What On Earth Are We Doing?*:

"Nowhere in the New Testament is there any call to believers to form a separate culture from the world. We were created to be separate from the world, but never to leave. Some Christians confuse 2 Corinthians 6:17 as a call to leave the world. Paul is talking about an internal, personal holiness, not a separate culture he want us to create, as if living in it will make us holy by osmosis. But in forming our own culture, all we have done is to leave the world without a witness from the inside, where we are supposed to be."

Are we as Native Christians guilty of having too small a view of God? Are we worshipping a culturally anemic God regarding our assumptions of how we believe God views our cultural forms and expressions? Is our God to small if we can't see Him working in our midst long before the European missionaries arrived? For many of us I believe I could safely say, we should answer "Yes" to most of the above questions.

I also believe, consequently, the reason 97% of our Native people are still without Christ is because we have rejected so much of our culture as Christians that we have been left without a witness from Jesus Christ from within the cultural contexts of our spiritual, traditional, and ceremonial life experiences. I have talked with Native believers who, because of these wrong assumptions, have become ostracized in their own communities because of their hard-line stance against their cultural traditions and are actually cultural outsiders themselves among their own people.

Syncretism – A Socio/cultural Definition

The issue of syncretism is a great concern for many of us in the Native work. I believe in order for syncretism to be accurately understood, it must be approached from a theological or doctrinal perspective, rather than a purely socio/cultural experientially-based one. By socio/cultural I simply mean a position or belief based on a person's subjective personal life experience – social and cultural. It seems many people today confuse the preferences and actual biblical error.

An example of socio/cultural would be seen in this story a Native woman told me. She said a Christian Native friend of hers had been experiencing some spiritual warfare and while praying felt the Holy Spirit revealed to her the entry point of this spiritual attack was the bracelet she was wearing. It contained some particular tribal designs. She felt to get rid of it. So she and two friends went to a nearby river and she tossed it out into the water. Shockingly, the bracelet then flew out of the water and landed at her feet on the shore. Yeehaw! They prayed again, with a little more fervor this time, and she threw it in again and it went away. Afterward the lady was fine and the warfare ceased. Do I believe this sort of thing happens? Absolutely! Do I believe that demonic spirits can somehow attach themselves to physical objects? I have no doubt.

Now let me explain how this personal experience can become a socio/cultural standard. Did the Holy Spirit reveal to the woman to get rid of Native bracelet? I have no reason to question that He did. Does the Bible prohibit the wearing of bracelets as jewelry? No. What about tribal or Native jewelry? No. But, because the Lord moved in her life in the particular way He did He did regarding her bracelet, these three ladies concluded that the wearing of ALL Native bracelets with similar tribal designs are demonized and should not be worn by Christians. Because of their personal subjective experience, they came to believe that to wear such things is syncretism and compromising of God's standards of holiness.

The fact is, not all Native bracelets with similar tribal designs are across-the-board evil. A Christian silversmith fashions a beautiful bracelet with traditional tribal designs that reflect his/her love of Christ and His creation. It has a distinct God-honoring meaning, but nearly identically resembles the designs of the bracelet thrown into the river.

A socio/cultural definition of syncretism says, because they are similar, they are identical and thus all bracelets with traditional Native designs cannot be worn. That belief is based purely on subjective personal experience, not revealed biblical doctrine and clear theology. It is an experienced-based position, a man-made one, not a biblical one.

Another example of socio/cultural standards regards the use of drums. In some parts of North America Native drums are to conjure up evil spirits. Human voices and animal sounds have been heard to come from a drum. Some Native believers then conclude that all Native drums are the property of the devil and are evil and can never be used for any purpose. This again becomes a standard based on a person's subjective experience not clear, biblical, guidelines and standards regarding music and musical instruments.

Which of your views and measures of our Native cultures are "man-based" vs. Bible-based? For example, where in the Book of Psalms can you point to and find God prohibiting the use of ceremony, dancing, drum playing, incense burning, assigning redemptive meaning to colors, and designing special articles of clothing for religious ceremony?

Syncretism – Some Theological Definitions

Lloyd Commander is the former Academic Dean of the Nazarene Indian Bible College in Alberqueque, and is currently Director of Education for the Confederated Tribes of the Umatilla. Lloyd has this to say about socio/cultural definitions of syncretism.

"Most people (Native) do not understand syncretism; therefore they hold on to what some highly esteemed leader or leaders (Native) have said in regards to its definition and expression. Also, it seems to me, this kind of reasoning is FEAR based. Fear has no place in the Jesus way. I believe it is a world-view carry-over from peoples' (Native) non-Christian background and also a way to control or try to control people because that is the way Christianity has been modeled to the Indian people."

Lloyd offered this definition of syncretism: "The union of two opposite forces, beliefs, systems or tenets so that the united form is a new thing, neither one nor the other."

Rev. Adrian Jacobs offers this definition of syncretism in his article titled, *Syncretism, Meeting of the Two Roads.* "Syncretism is the attempted union of different or opposing principles or practices. Trying to marry two different and even opposing philosophies or religions. Without qualitfication, the syncretist says that the assumption can be made that because the two are similar, they are the same –synonymous."

Robert Schreiter, theologian and American missiologist, states the commonly understood definition of syncretism as "a distorted form of Christian faith, skewed by cultural and religious forces in the environment into which Christianity has come." Robert J.Schreiter, "Defining Syncretism: An Interim Reports," *International Bulletin of Missionary Research* 17/2 (1993),pg.50

The Native American Church would be an example of this. In their services they use the Bible and sing Christian songs. Yet the one thing that sets them apart is their prescribed use of the hallucinogenic drug found in peyote as part of their liturgy. The peyote is intended to increase one's receptiveness to God and therefore make the participant more holy and closer to God as a result. They have attempted to form one new religion out of two that is neither Christian nor traditionally Native. This is syncretism.

Syncretism – A Cultural Reality in North America

I want to make a very clear distinction and separation here between doctrinal and cultural syncretism. Our theological concern is with what we have been discussing, religious or doctrinal syncretism, the mixing or joining together on non-biblical religious belief systems with historic Christianity.

Cultural syncretism is a normal fact of life. America is the epitome of cultural syncretism. It is called the "melting pot" of the world because it is a blend or mixture of the cultural expression of the peoples of the earth. The entire population of North America is comprised solely of immigrants from other countries (First Nations are less than 1%). American and Canadian culture is a unique blend of the languages, music and dance, art, economic systems, political structures, technology, sciences, etc. of its citizens. Culturally speaking, then, America is a syncretistic nation.

The English word "syncretism" has the same Latin root from which we get the words "synergy" and "syncopation."

In the history of our tribes, we often exchanged songs, ceremonies, values, weapons, and artifacts that were unique to a geographic region. When horses were introduced in the Plains by the Spanish, the cultures and lifestyle of the first tribes to acquire them were radically altered. They often went from sedentary agrarian societies to nomadic, warrior hunters. The horse was far more than a beast of burden; it represented a way of life. In terms of its effect on the Plains' tribes, it was "advanced technology and industry" at its finest. When introduced through trade to other tribes, horses became an immeasurable catalyst of cultural transformation. This is another example of cultural syncretism. A mixing or blending of two cultural lifestyles that becomes something previously unknown.

So then, is there a theological problem with combining the cultural forms and expressions of different nations and peoples in Christian faith?

Syncretism – Some Theological Reflections

I have made a distinction between cultural and religious/doctrinal syncretism. Let me define what I believe the critical issue is regarding religious/doctrinal syncretism, which is what I believe we should be primarily concerned about.

I would like to suggest that syncretism is much more than an application, misuse or practice of a particular form, i.e. music, musical instruments, language, dance, custom, social practice, ceremony, art, etc. Nor is it simply the combining of, or use of similar or even identical ceremonial forms, methods or liturgies.

Syncretism is a theological issue of faith and allegiance, not merely wedding religious forms.

Because a satanist burns candles purchased at a department store for his animal sacrifices, it doesn't make us syncretists to burn the similar candles purchased at the same department store during our New Year's service. Theologically speaking, because a shaman uses an elk hide hand drum to conjure evil spirits, it doesn't make me a syncretist to use my elk hide drum to honor Christ and the Holy Spirit on Sunday morning in church. I want to submit to you for your consideration, what I believe are some solid biblical perspectives for syncretism.

Syncretism is a belief or practice, whether in an Anglo Church on Sunday morning or a Native ceremony, that attempts to replace or distort the historical doctrines of justification, righteousness, atonement, holiness, redemption, sanctification, salvation, etc. It is anything that tries to replace, augment or add to the longstanding doctrines of historical Christianity.

Syncretism is any belief or practice that says Christ's work alone is not enough.

Syncretism, as we are defining it, is not baptizing in a creek or bathtub. Syncretism is not meeting at an Elks Lodge, using a hand drum, playing an electric guitar on Sunday morning, worshipping singing traditional Choctaw hymns, wearing a ribbon shirt, wearing an eagle, turkey, or pigeon feather, owning a television, listening to a non-Christian CD or sleeping in a tipi.

Biblically speaking, it is not necessarily owning a dream catcher, attending a give-away (potlatch) to honor a relative, attending or dancing in a pow-wow, square dancing or hanging a buffalo skull in your living room, or even burning a stick of raspberry incense or braid of sage or sweet grass. Like throwing horse's milk up in the air, there is no biblical prohibition against doing any of these things. In the light of the definition of syncretism we are working with, doing these things is not necessarily being syncretistic or compromising God's Word or my Christian testimony.

Syncretism is believing that by performing a particular religious ceremony, or practice, one can alters the essential human spiritual condition in the same way that Jesus does, through His death on a cross, burial, and resurrection from the dead; and continues by faith to accomplish in the lives of believers today.

Theologically, syncretism is saying a Native ceremony can cleanse the soul from sin in the same way the blood of Jesus does; or that performing ceremonial laws can bridge the sin barrier separating a holy God and sinful man. It is assigning the same weight of power and authority to Native religion and ceremony that you do to the revelation of truth found in the Word of God. This is syncretism and biblical error.

It would be my opinion that a primary cause of the lack of Christianity's impact on tribal people has to do with a condescending approach to and rejection of the notion of God's creative sovereignty in the cultural expressions of life and worship among First Nations people. Unfortunately as a consequence of this, our problem today is no longer a misguided white missionary, but the erroneous teaching of that long-ago missionary that has been adopted by us as Native leaders as a "Native perspective."

What we are left with by this lingering centuries-old paternalism as Native Christians is a fear, distrust, suspicion, alienation, and rejection of much of our own culture as followers of Christ.

As Native leaders it is we who must be careful that we do not allow an emphasis on subjective personal experience and not solid biblical theology, to lead us unfounded fear of syncretism among ourselves. We must counsel, pray, and dialogue to prevent syncretism from becoming an emotionally defined standard that will only lead to more confusion, division, and lack of ministry effectiveness among us. When we try to artificially separate Native believers from their cultural practices and traditions, we are actually denying God's creative handiwork is us.

The end result is, we can't see the design or plan of God in our cultural identities as First Nations people – Navajo, Kiowa, Apache, Sioux, etc., even though we readily embrace the cultural expressions of Holland, England, Germany, and France.

What we're after is authentic and legitimate Christian expressions coming from aboriginal peoples, the Indigenous Church."

This is an abbreviated version of Dr. Twiss' article on syncretism. For the full article see his book, *Many Tribes, One Church,* available at WICONI,

P.O.Box 5246 Vancouver, WA 98668

Appendix F

Additional Resources

The Sentinel Group (George and Lisa Otis)

P.O.Box 6334 - Lynnwood, WA 98036

Books – *Informed Intercession, The Twilight Labyrinth*

Teachings and videos

Aloha Ke Akua (Daniel Kikawa)

HC 2 Box 6845

Kea'au, HI 96749

Book – *Perpetuated in Righeousness*

WICONI (Dr. Richard and Kathryn Twiss)

P.O.Box 5246
Vancouver, WA 98668

Book – *Many Tribes, One Church* and others

Windwalkers Int'l. (Rev. Mary Glazier)

4731 Mars Dr.

Anchorage, AK 99507

Many teaching resources on intercession etc.

Indigenous Messengers Int'l. (Rev. Qaumaniq and Dr. Suuqiina)

P.O.Box 1088

Victorville, CA 92393 www.IndigenousMessengers.com

Appendix G

IMI Resources

IndigenousMessengers.com

Books

Warfare By Honor

Restoring Honor Through Protocol

His Glorious Names

365 Hebrew names of YHWH

DVD's

Warfare By Honor

Protocol -4 DVD's

The Olive Tree-Romans 11

Malachi

Freedom From Toxic Systems

Restoration of Women

The Restoration of Women-3 DVD's

Hebrew Idioms

Opening the Scrolls

The End Times

Where Are the Bees

Ten Native Values

CD's

Let's Fly (original music)

YHWH's Names as Ringtones for cell phones

I Lay Me Down-Ps.23 (original music)

Ministry

Dr. Suuqiina is available for teaching venues including churches, seminars, conferences, home meetings, camps, retreats, and gatherings.

Contact IMI at 615-424-7948

ndigenus@cs.com

www.IndigenousMessengers.com